HOME FORGOTTEN

THE CAMPBELLS OF THE NORTH RIVER

REVIEWS

Never before has such a documentary of a singular Ohio family touched so many aspects of American history. This is a fascinating account of a family with conviction to the cause of abolishing slavery as well as changing the face of the iron industry, education and medicine. The obviously well-researched family history by a direct descendant has resulted in a great early American adventure.

Lee Edwards, Curator
Ripley Museum, Ripley, Ohio
Historian of Rev. John Rankin

The Campbell family history is a fascinating detective story that takes the reader and family genealogist on a journey from frontier hardships to industrial entrepreneurship. An infinite amount of painstaking research and historical sleuthing have turned a bare-bones genealogy into a colorful and true story that is more than just a recitation of birth and death dates. In fact the Campbell story is the American story. Along the way, the author is not afraid to engage in a little myth-busting as he brings his own family history to light in an organized and engaging manner.

Nancy Sorrells
Chair, Augusta County Board
of Commissioners
Past-President, Augusta County
Historical Society

HOME FORGOTTEN

THE CAMPBELLS OF THE NORTH RIVER

REV. JAMES A. CAMPBELL, D. MIN.

Eagle River, Alaska

Copyright © 2007 by Rev. James A. Campbell, D. Min.

All rights reserved. No part of this book may be reproduced in any form without permission except by a reviewer who may quote brief passages in a media review.

Photo Credits:	Briggs-Lawrence County Library, Ironton, Ohio
	Mason County Historical Society, Maysville, Kentucky
	Lawrence County Historical Society, Ironton, Ohio
	State Historical Society of Iowa, Des Moines, Iowa
	Cincinnati Historical Society, Cincinnati, Ohio
	Library of Congress, Washington, D.C.
	Nancy Sorells
	Dr. Allan C. Campbell, M.D.
	Personal collection of author
News Article:	The Ironton Tribune, Ironton, Ohio
Portrait:	Carolyn Von Stein
Poetry:	Lydia H. Sigourney
	M. B. Crocker

Published by:

NORTHBOOKS
17050 N. Eagle River Loop Road, # 3
Eagle River, Alaska 99577
www.northbooks.com

Printed in the United States of America

ISBN 978-0-9789766-4-4

Library of Congress Control Number: 2007928839

Dedication

Dedicated to the memory

of

Eloise Campbell

and in appreciation to

Dr. Allan and Marlene Campbell

*for their encouragement and support
through the long journey of writing this book.*

Contents

Foreword . . . . *ix*

Preface . . . . *xi*

Acknowledgments . . . . *xiii*

The Old, Old Story *1*

> Earliest recorded ancestors....Duncan (Scotland)....Children....Dougel....Robert....John....Variations of accounts of the arrival and lineage of the Campbells to Virginia.

A History For Our Times *11*

> Revision of earlier family histories....The North River of the Shenandoah as the Campbell home of Robert and sons Charles, Hugh, and John....The birth of the first American generations.

But Who Were They? *19*

> Life on the North River....New Light Presbyterians....Family economics....Campbells in the Revolution....Mary Trotter Campbell....Touring the Campbell lands.

William and Elizabeth Wilson Campbell *40*

> Following the line of Charles' youngest son William....Genealogical problems....The life of William Campbell....Planning and moving to Kentucky....Hard times at Blue Licks, Kentucky....Moving on to Ohio.

Ohio *54*

> Locating the Ohio homestead of William and Elizabeth Campbell....Life on the Ohio frontier....The grown children of William and Elizabeth Campbell....William Campbell's church trial.

John W. Campbell *62*

> Entering law....The War of 1812....Ohio Legislature....Serving in the U.S. House of Representatives....Running for Governor of Ohio....U.S. federal judge for Ohio.

Charles Campbell *74*

> Charles, second son of William....Sons of Charles and Elizabeth....James M. and William W. and the founding of Morton, Illinois....John C. Campbell, iron industrialist....building with William Firmstone the first iron hot blast furnace in America....The founding of Ironton, Ohio....Joseph N. H. "Harvey" Campbell, Iowa legislator.

Joseph N. Campbell *102*

Youngest son of William and Elizabeth, Ripley Merchant....Father of William B. Campbell....family line of Dr. Elizabeth Campbell and M. Edith Campbell....The life and accomplishments of the Campbell sisters of Cincinnati.

James W. Campbell *122*

Oldest son of William and Elizabeth....Marries Mary "Polly" Duncan daughter of frontiersman David Duncan....James Campbell's farming operation and manufacture of "wheat fans"....Spiritual values....The children of James W. and Mary Campbell....The four daughters....Hiram Campbell, ironmaster with cousin John Campbell in Ironton, Ohio....John Milton Campbell, missionary to Africa....Washington G. Campbell, land appraiser.

Abolition *166*

Campbell family parishioners of abolitionists Rev. John Rankin and Rev. James Gilliland....Colonization and John W. Campbell....Internal family struggles with abolition....The role and influence of John Milton Campbell in abolition.... John Campbell and Hiram Campbell and abolition in Ironton....The impact of abolition on the work of M. Edith and Elizabeth Campbell in Cinicnnati.

Notable Exceptions *191*

Phoebe Campbell Martin, the Campbell family that remained in Brown County.... Son William Campbell Martin....Son Rev. John Martin....The Campbell Cousins of Ripley....Charles Fenelon Campbell and family.

Home Forgotten *200*

The disconnect....Everything but the faintest details of this book is lost to memory....Why did this happen?

The Last Home Place *203*

Washington G. Campbell and Eleanor J. Campbell move to Illinois.... Homesteading, land speculating and deep personal loss....The trials and revelations of the settlement of Washington's estate....Son James M. and Sarah Cook Campbell carry on the family farming operation....The early death of Sarah Campbell and its impact on the family....The death of James M. Campbell and the family migration to Iowa....Efforts to stay connected as a family....The Campbells during the depression....Clair and Eloise Campbell and the birth of son Allan C. Campbell....memories of the last home place.

Discovery *231*

Grandchildren of James M. Campbell and Sarah Campbell gathering for reunion in 1963....Graduate School at the University of Illinois and meeting my Illinois Campbell cousins....The beginnings of the thirty-year search for our Campbell roots....Dr. Allan C. Campbell pursues his own interests in history....The great family road trip home to Ironton in 1999.

The blessing to our children.

Foreword

"The simple wooden box that contained the belongings of Rev. John Milton Campbell was shipped home from Africa to his mother Mary and she carried them with her out west to Illinois. The next generation, however, did not see the worth of holding on to such items.... Except for the candlestick holder that was pretty, the rest was thrown away," writes James Campbell of his discoveries amidst the texts and forgotten family relicts as he traveled through Virginia, Kentucky, Ohio, and Illinois in search of his Scottish ancestral New World transplants of the 1740s. A hundred years have dusted in oblivion his family's "promise of the new."

Through his meticulous research, wrought with miracle discoveries, the Campbell family travails across the early Midwest countryside now have come to life. Moreover, in his personal quest James Campbell has unwittingly unveiled a generous regional portion of our national history.

While he retraces the footsteps of his own kin, James Campbell also shifts the dust of the uncountable parallel footsteps of other European settlers in the New World. It is through the affectionate personal curiosity over our origins that his efforts yield an unexpected discovery and add scientific credence to the myth and the lore which surround the birth cradle of our nation. James Campbell's efforts yield a wealth of knowledge to the forging of the U.S.A—ab urbe condito.

His comments and observations add an interesting personal aspect to this fascinating chronicle of events, imbuing the narrative with a compelling emotional subtext. Many others should follow his path, passion and diligence, if not to search for their own roots, then, at least to admire the details in the life of one settler family, and in so doing, to affirm the roots of our American self-determination, and fortitude in becoming a free nation.

Danuta Zamojska Hutchins

Author of *Torn Out Memories;* retired Professor of Languages, Literatures, and Cultures; former Visiting Professor at Ohio State University, Columbus, Ohio.

Preface

WHY THIS BOOK MATTERS

Home Forgotten began as an essay for my children. It would be ten pages, twenty pages at most. It would be a collective picture of ancestors in the great mass of other farm families working the land and moving on. With a little luck I would find out, at least in general, where in Ohio and Kentucky they came from. It probably would take me a year.

It has taken thirty years.

What became a search for names and places became a search for persons behind the names, persons who would play a valued role in the unfolding of the Ohio territory. The search for family became the telling of the settling of the Ohio Valley through one family's eyes. A family history fast became a regional history of industry, politics, religion, medicine and education.

In time the work became more that a regional history. It became a statement about history. History is told by those who stay behind, those who identify with the region and thus tell the story and give identity to a region. Those who move on are often forgotten. The Campbells of the North River, at least in Augusta County, Virgina, and later in Brown County, Ohio, were a family forgotten. They moved on and their legacy splintered into notable fragments that in time became even forgotten to themselves, at least until now.

This work serves as a model of what is yet to be found many times over of families that move on, families forgotten in every region of the country. We are at the beginning of a new age of retelling regional histories. Much of this is due to Internet connections not only to professional genealogical resources but to families seeking their way home.

At the same time the book serves as a red flag to the liabilities of Internet family research. Online misinformation abounds until it becomes an unchecked genealogical virus. Family stories are not increasingly true simply because the same lineage is repeated twenty times over on the same genealogical website. Family research on the Internet is a double-edge sword and this work underlines both the potential for research to track down the forgotten and the discernment of misinformation that needs to be forgotten.

This work also is an example of the impact of a region far beyond its horizons of time and place. Through this one family's migrations we see afresh how the moral groundings of the abolitionist movement in Brown County were extended in ways and places not considered before.

Finally, the issue of forgetting. This book is a testament of how history is forgotten and how terribly hard it is to be reclaimed. How fragile our awareness is of the past. We watch on Antique Road Show as items worth thousands of dollars are bought for pennies at a garage sale. We see the wonder in people's faces as they discover what treasures they have purchased for nothing. We need also remember that these same treasures were not just found, they were first discarded. They were dismissed to the rummage sale not only because the owner failed to see their worth, but because that person had perhaps lost connection, reverence to the antiques story. It happens all the time; we not only squander priceless heirlooms but the sacred, life giving, spiritual story of our connection to who our family once was.

Danuta Hutchins in her Foreword, lifted from the book's text the primary image that captured the moment of our family's disconnect and gave the book its title. It is repeated for emphasis. It is the iconic image at the soul and title of this book.

The simple wooden box that contained the belongings of Rev. John Milton Campbell was shipped home from Africa to his mother Mary and she carried them with her out west to Illinois. The next generation, however, did not see the worth of holding on to such items…. Except for the candlestick holder that was pretty, the rest was thrown away.

Acknowledgments

VIRGINIA: Katherine Bushman, Nancy Sorrells (Staunton, Virginia), Lucille Balfour (Hugh Campbell line), Carol Gilmour (South Carolina), Richmond: The Library of Virginia, The Virginia Historical Society,

KENTUCKY: Jean Calvert, Maysville Historical Society, Caren Dawn Curotto.

PENNSYLVANIA: The Canal Historical Society. The Historical Society of Easton.

OHIO: Ironton: Virginia Bryant, The Lawrence County Historical Society. Briggs Library, Ironton. Jan Rader, Olive Furnace photos. Ripley: Rankin Historical site, Dee Puff, Dorothy Helton, Lee Edwards, Mary Martin Bick, Pat Donaldson, Teresa Robinson and Melody Kokensparger of Family Matters Research, Ripley. Ohio State Historical Society, Columbus, Western Reserve Historical Society, Cleveland. Lynn Gardner, Georgetown, The Cincinnati Historical Society, Carol Maher, Cincinnati Public Library.

ILLINOIS: Morton: Ruth and Donald Roth, Mary Fouts, Champaign-Urbana: Urbana Free Library Archives Department, Carolyn Adams, Archive Assistant, Eloise Campbell,

Ruby Campbell Phd., Genealogist, Clan Campbell Society of North America

Chapter One

The Old, Old Story

THE HISTORY OF 1828

It happened on Monday, May 12, 1828, in Brown County, Ohio, just outside of Georgetown on the Charles Campbell farm.[1] That is when and where Charles Campbell told the story, the story of the Campbells of the North River. He told it to his son John who transcribed his father's memories. Charles was not the first to tell the family story. Brother John W. Campbell, U.S. Congressman and soon to be U.S. federal judge for Ohio, loved to tell a form of the story again and again, especially as political fodder to note his rise from noble but humble beginnings. Other members of the extended family were professional historians and became, for their day, the authorities on the history of Virginia. Certainly they had the Campbell connection to the larger sweep of the birth of the nation. Still, if such family stories were committed to paper they have been lost to time.

May 12, 1828—that was when the story gelled into history and none too soon. It was nearly a century since the family arrived in Virginia. The family had since moved twice. Charles Campbell's father William, who fought in the Revolution, had died six years before. History distorts quickly with the loss of details, the blur of events, the adding of embellishment.

Still, in 1828, Charles' mother Elizabeth was alive and there were ten brothers and sisters within ten miles to verify any concern for details, and the connections back to Augusta County, Virginia, were still viable. The history of 1828 had the potential for authority and we are told that history was extensive. It was also handed on to Charles' grandson and was a primary resource when the grandson set the family history to print in 1911. But what happened to the 1828 history? Such a prized possession would have been given to someone or some institution that would have treasured its worth.

The search for that history has covered years with the passion of one looking for the Holy Grail. Nothing. Maybe one day it will turn up. That day will be a celebration. In the meantime, we are left to sift the stories of the 1911 history and discern what probably came from that early transcription of 1828. Still, such educated guessing is just that—except for a letter written by the grandson of Charles Campbell to a Miss Lettie Green of Danville, Kentucky, September 24, 1907.[2]

In the letter the grandson of Charles Campbell was weighing the pedigree chart of the Campbells of the North River against the pedigree chart of another Campbell family of Augusta County, Virginia. He commented on his family pedigree as he went along, but he outlined the pedigree *as it was given to him*. Putting the comments in the margins aside, the bare-bone family tree is as close as we will get to the handed-on history of 1828. This family tree diagram of 1907 is the earliest diagram we have of our family lineage (shown on page 3).

WHAT CAN WE LEARN FROM THIS FAMILY TREE?

The Campbells of the North River were descendants from a Duncan Campbell whose wife is unknown.

This Duncan never left Scotland. His three sons, Dougal, Robert, and John Campbell, moved to Coleraine in County Derry, Northern Ireland in 1700.

Shortly after moving to Coleraine, Robert's three sons were born: Hugh, John, and Charles. All three of Robert's sons immigrated to America.

The Old, Old Story

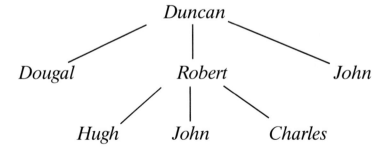

The family lineage of the Campbells of the North River copied from the letter to Lettie Green, September 24, 1907

Again, everything else on this chart is added comment to be considered in the second telling of the story. Holding our focus to these bare-bone facts alone, the family lineage begins as follows:

```
                Duncan
         /        |         \
    Dougal     Robert        John
             /   |   \
          Hugh  John  Charles
```

THE HISTORY OF 1911

The name of the grandson who inherited the history of 1828 has been withheld for a reason. The name of the grandson is Charles, named for the one from which the history of 1828 came, even as that Charles was the grandson of Charles Campbell who immigrated to America.

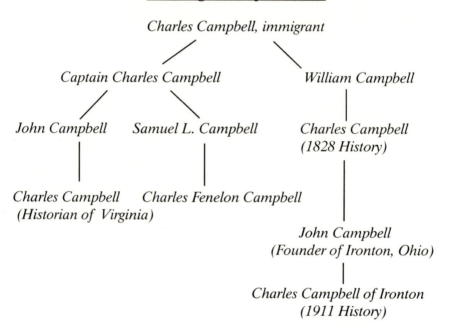

The Legacies of Charles

There are so many Charles Campbells in the first four generations in America it becomes overwhelming to the casual reader. For now we focus on three Charles Campbells:

1. Charles the immigrant to Virginia born in 1703.

2. Charles the son of William and grandson of the immigrant who gave the history of 1828.

3. Charles of Ironton, Ohio, the grandson of the Charles who told the history of 1828. Charles of Ironton wrote the family history of 1911.

The Old, Old Story

Charles of Ironton, Ohio, was the son of John Campbell who founded Ironton. Charles was an engineer and knew how to research. He had a passion and long-term commitment to genealogy, and by 1900 had gathered thirty years of family anecdotes and memorabilia. Most of all, Charles of Ironton knew how to make connections to other family genealogists and he knew how to blend histories together.

Of particular mention is the blending of the history of 1828 written down by his father John and the history of the family from his father's brother, Uncle James M. Campbell of Morton, Illinois. It was Uncle James who not only has the lineage of the ancestors but the details that made the story come alive. Unfortunately, this written history by Uncle James has been lost to time as well—that is except for the quotes that found their way into the blended history of Charles Campbell of Ironton, Ohio.

By 1900 an emerging assumption was taking place among people researching the founding Campbells of Augusta County. A consensus brewed that all the Campbells who settled Augusta County, Virginia, were of one extended family unit: descendants of a Duncan Campbell whom they believed was married to a Mary McCoy. From this assumption came a book, the very mention of which brings frustration and caution to many modern researchers. The book is Margaret Campbell Pilcher's *Historical Sketches of the Campbell, Pilcher and Kindred Families,* published in 1911. For several years the premises, inconsistencies, and omissions of this book were a continual focus of research of the Clan Campbell Society of North America. Indeed, for a while a full ten percent of inquiries to the clan genealogist were from people seeking more information on this line of the Campbells of Augusta County, Virginia.[3]

In the very middle of this controversial book is a single extended essay on the Campbells of the North River by Charles Campbell of Ironton, Ohio.[4] Charles was determined in his

Charles Campbell of Ironton, Ohio, whose 1911 family history was the first published account of the Campbells of the North River
Photo courtesy of Briggs-Lawrence County Library, Ironton, Ohio

The Old, Old Story

essay to show how the North River families must relate to the Campbells of south Augusta County in Beverley Manor that were the primary focus of the book. It almost fits—but not quite. There were several leaps of faith. Still, because it was close enough, the long essay of the story of our family made it into print in the Pilcher book. Regardless of whether such connection is valid, we are grateful that Margaret Campbell Pilcher let Charles Campbell include the story of his family line in her book. Without this book we would have lost not two, but three histories of our family. And so, what do we learn from the history of 1911?

Charles Campbell of Ironton tells us that sons of Robert Campbell of Coleraine, Northern Ireland, Hugh and Charles Campbell, arrived in Augusta County, Virginia, in 1740. Public record affirms that Hugh Campbell proved his importation in June of that year.[5] To prove one's importation was to indicate one came to the colonies at their own expense. This also gave them privilege of fifty acres of free land per family member. Hugh was traveling with wife Esther Magill Campbell and their daughter Sarah. So Hugh received one hundred fifty acres of free land beyond whatever land he purchased on his own.

According to Charles Campbell of Ironton, the Campbells did not settle on the North River as the title of the book suggests but on the Middle River of the headwaters of the Shenandoah River. This assumption was made on the grounds that the Campbells were neighbors to the James Anderson family and the Andersons lived on the Middle River near the Old Stone Church.

The history of 1911 then asserts that immigrant Charles Campbell no sooner became established in Augusta County, Virginia, than he and his family joined fellow immigrant James Anderson in an enormous land investment opportunity in Pendleton, South Carolina.

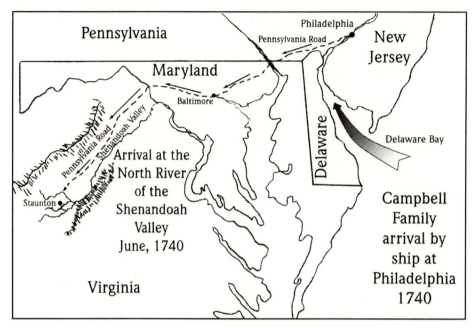

Migratory route of most of the Scot-Irish settlement in early Augusta County, Virginia

Here, Charles of Ironton quotes directly from Uncle James M. Campbell:

> *Charles Campbell and Mary Trotter Campbell at one time lived in South Carolina. Just prior to the depreciation of Continental money, he sold his land for 8,000 pounds equal then to $25,000.00 [value of dollar in 1911] and came to near Grattan Mills and Millar Iron Works. In Augusta County Virginia…. the depreciation of currency just after the sale caused him some loss. He probably returned to Augusta County in 1746, disposing of his South Carolina property long after it had enhanced in value.*
>
> *He, [Charles] was a planter with numerous slaves. In Virginia he lived in a large fine house, the first story of stone, the second of logs. We can imagine the house so built, because of the Indians.[6]*

The Old, Old Story

The focus of the 1911 history dwelled on the Campbell family's means and influence. It was a premise fueled further by a new-found connection that answered the question, "What happened to the third immigrant brother, Charles' and Hugh's brother, John?"

Charles of Ironton was certain that the John Campbell who married Elizabeth Walker had to be the missing brother John. This John Campbell came with his Walker inlaws to the colonies in the late 1720s. What is more, this John Campbell claimed he was of the Campbells of Kirnan, Scotland, living in exile as the rightful heir of the lands of the Duke of Argyle. If this John could prove one last connection to the family line, he would inherit a fortune set aside for him in the British treasury.

Of course if John were next in line as the Duke of Argyle, then brothers Charles and Hugh would have at least known about it and it would have been mentioned as a part of the story handed on. It wasn't. It was evident that even as Charles of Ironton writes his history believing this immigrant John was the brother of Hugh and Charles, this John might have also been a bit over the top. The history of 1911 states, "...the earliest family records often transmit to us that which may be of value, and can not be irreverently ignored, yet it does not command our implicit confidence. ....we are all warned that the lure of the dollar is present with us, because of the traditional estate (of Scotland) paid into the English treasury for lack of heirs, a fortune as elusive as will-o-the-wisp."[7]

If such a story of noble birth and elusive fortune is suspect, it was not without correlation to stories of noble ancestry in the oral history of the North River Campbells. Supposedly, immigrant Charles Campbell had in his possession a chair with the hilt of a sword imbedded in the back. The sword was a gift from King William of Orange for an ancestor's participation in the Battle of the Boyne in 1692. Such an unusual family heirloom seems plausible but not verifiable. It too, if it existed, is a piece of lost history.[8]

For all the blending of stories found in the history of 1911, the blending did not include much verification with public record. History was what grandma or grandpa, father and uncle said it was and carried the authority of tribute paid to the elders of the family, especially if they wrote it down, particularly if they wrote it down in the family Bible. By the mid-nineteenth century a romantic, larger than life general view of the founding of America was complemented by individual families claiming status by connection to the founding of the nation. It was an atmosphere that lent itself to exaggeration and sometimes leaps of faith in making connections to family that have no merit. We will see just how much such distortions can impact history in a chapter that follows.

What matters now is to sift the fragments of the history of 1828, reminiscences of Uncle James Campbell, and the blended history of 1911 against the public record of Augusta County, Virginia. More, we apply on-line resources including the original public documents available through the Library of Virginia. We consider the results of hired regional historians and the findings of scholars who provide in-depth analysis of life in Augusta County in the mid-1700s. What emerges is the story of the Campbells of the North River for our day and the foundation for the next generation to begin its work.

Chapter Two

A History For Our Times

Her name was Katherine Bushman. For decades she was the leading authority on family history in Augusta County, Virginia. The website of the Augusta County Historical Society is dedicated to her honor. The research she leaves behind is the core of modern family research in the region. It was to her that two questions were posed in 1984: Which Charles Campbell of Augusta County is ours and where exactly on the Middle River of the Shenandoah did he live? With this request Katherine Bushman received a copy of the history of 1911, the work of Charles Campbell of Ironton.

Katherine Bushman's response: There were two Charles Campbells in Augusta County in the 1740s. There was the Charles Campbell of South Augusta County and the Charles Campbell of the North River. There was no Charles Campbell on the Middle River. Just because Charles Campbell bought his land from James Anderson who lived on the Middle River, does not mean they were neighbors. James Anderson owned many parcels of land and the one he sold to Charles Campbell was further north than the 1911 history portrayed.[1]

Now it made sense. In the 1911 history mention is made that the Augusta County landmarks for the Campbells were Millers Iron Works and Gratten Mills. For Charles of Ironton they seemed oddly too far north in Augusta County to be landmarks for the family farm. Still, they must have been the only landmarks available.[2] No, they were landmarks because the family lived near those landmarks on the North River. They are the Campbells of the North River.

The importance of locating the family lands on the North River cannot be stressed enough. Not only was immigrant

11

Charles Campbell living on the North River, but he and his family and brother Hugh and his family were a part of the North River community, a settlement unto itself that was the focus of the extensive research of C.E. May culminating in his work *Life Under Four Flags in the North River Basin*. Opening that volume was a trip back in time to the earliest years of the Campbell family in America.

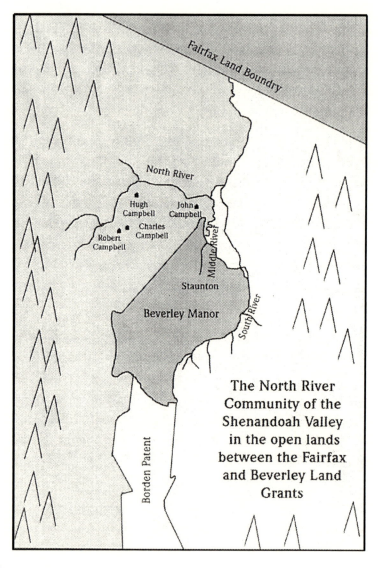

The North River Community of the Shenandoah Valley in the open lands between the Fairfax and Beverley Land Grants

Finding this discrepancy gave reason to take a closer look at each premise of the Campbell legacy beginning with the assumption that the family came to America from Coleraine in County Derry in Northern Ireland. To prove this by public record would require a significant investment and the right researcher in Northern Ireland. With deep gratitude to my cousin Dr. Allan Campbell, who underwrote the research, we were able to hire John McCabe, the dean of family research in Northern Ireland.

We knew such an investigation was a long shot. Public records of that time are sparse. Only the few "landed" persons of means were found on public ledgers. Still, if the Campbells came by their own means to America and then invested well in the Carolinas, they must have been people of means in Ireland.

At first the research proved exciting. We had found through McCabe a Robert Campbell of Coleraine. In fact, we found detailed drawings of the town that showed the very house in which Robert Campbell lived. The imagination was kindled red hot by the early returns of information from Ireland.

Few dead ends of research provided so much wonder and so much despair. Soon things began to not fit. This Robert Campbell of Coleraine lived well into the 1770s and died in Coleraine. Our Robert Campbell, father of Charles, Hugh, and John was beginning to show up on Augusta County Records in the 1750s.[3] Robert dies in Virginia in 1768.[4] In fact, there was no other reference to a Robert, Charles, or Hugh Campbell that even closely matched our family in all of County Derry during the years they were supposed to be living there.[5]

It was in this dry well of research that new insight emerged of the family's Ireland years. The oral history of the family stated that Charles Campbell married Mary Trotter in Ireland in 1735. Hugh Campbell married Esther Magill in Ireland as well. Mary Trotter and Esther Magill were not from Coleraine or even County Derry or surrounding counties. They were both from County Down 110 miles to the southeast. In those days people married persons within ten to twenty miles of home. To have not one but both brothers marry women from County Down seemed more than just coincidence. Furthermore, the high percentage of people who immigrated to the lands around the Campbells on the North River were from County Down.

Thus, the likelihood is that if the Campbells once lived in Coleraine, they probably moved to County Down by the 1730s and they most likely left for America as part of a migration of County Down people. It is also possible that the last place the ship to America docked in Northern Ireland was Coleraine. Such association with the last port of call before the colonies is not uncommon.

Now we consider the second issue. After the Campbells came to Augusta County, Virginia, in 1740, son Charles and family moved shortly thereafter to Pendleton, South Carolina.

To verify this claim, researcher Carole Gilmour of South Carolina was hired to comb the public records. Nothing showed. This is particularly puzzling mindful of such a large land transaction that certainly would have made public record. Wrote Carole Gilmore, "Although many smaller transactions were not recorded, especially up here on the frontier, a land transaction as large as the one mentioned in the Campbell book would have certainly been recorded...it would have been important to have sound title to such a large tract of land as the one that we are talking about."[6]

Of further concern is that in 1742, Charles and Hugh Campbell both showed up for the muster of the Augusta County Militia.[7] In June of 1745, Charles Campbell had land surveyed in the North River region[8] as well as the next year and the year after that. If Charles Campbell went to South Carolina it would have had to have been between 1742 and 1745. For such commitment it didn't match.

What are we to do with this? The story of the sojourn to South Carolina has too many details to be dismissed. Oral tradition, however blurred, has a way of coming around. Perhaps there is something that happened but it wasn't showing on public record. Perhaps the story may have been misconstrued to a different time. Descendants of Charles Campbell did migrate to South Carolina in 1767, though certainly not with the wealth the story suggests.

Next is the matter of the Charles Campbell home with numerous slaves and a large fine house with the first floor of stone and the second of logs for protection.

It would be difficult to challenge this description mindful that the Charles Campbell who gave the oral history of 1828 was born in the house and lived there until he was fourteen. Indeed, as we shall see the homes of both Hugh and Charles were noted as plantations with very large acreages. Such a home, however, needs to be weighed on its own terms, in its own location.

Indeed the Campbells, both Charles and Hugh, had slaves but even a few slaves in Augusta County in the 1750s were a luxury. Augusta County was poor, poor for everyone including the more fortunate. Augusta County was the only region in the state where both slave and slave master and his family worked together in the fields. When grandfather Robert Campbell died in 1768 he left an estate that included six slaves.[9] Six slaves for that time was indeed "many"—at least for Augusta County. By the measure of other locales it was modest.

In like measure, when Charles Campbell died in 1778 the assessment of his estate amounted to more than average but nothing of extravagance. The more exceptional items of his belongings included: one walnut table with six chairs, one pine table, one pine chest, three beds, two of them with furniture, four pewter dishes, ten soup plates, five wooden plates, six spoons, two china dishes, four china plates, one stone mug, one tea cup and saucer, three pots, one large oven, one pail and dish, and four basins. Charles also had two changes of clothes including a blue coat and jacket, a black coat and jacket and a pair of stockings. If there was any measure of privilege in Charles life it was his small "library" of nine books.[10]

We also note with this that at one point Charles owned 1,236 acres of land. Brother Hugh owned 1,386 acres. Together that is 2,624 acres. Even by today's standards that is a significant farming operation. Most farms in Augusta County in the 1700s were between 100 and 500 acres. Still much of the land held by the Campbells was most likely kept to be sold to other immigrants to pay taxes. What land was left of the Charles Campbell plantation by 1770 was divided up among the several sons of the family. At the end of his life Charles was living on a single farmstead of 220 acres that surrounded the family home.

Augusta County was the frontier. The Campbells fared all right in circumstances that were harsh and demanding. It was a circumstance captured in 1796 by La Rochefoucauld-Liancourt, "There were no rich planters in the upper part of the Shenandoah Valley and therefore relatively few Negroes yet all these petty planters, however poor or wretched, apparently have one slave who shares their toils and distresses."[11]

Yes, it may have been a large fine house, in comparison. There may have been many slaves, in comparison. They had privilege, in comparison. The key word is comparison and we will pursue the meaning of the comparison of wealth in the next chapter. For now the word is used to qualify the history of 1911.

Finally, there is the issue of the third brother, John Campbell. It is frustrating that brother John Campbell does not show up on the will of father Robert Campbell in 1768. Charles signs and Hugh signs, but not John. There is no record of John on any family transaction—except one. The very first family land survey in Virginia was made by Charles Campbell in June 1745, for a tract of land on the Pennsylvania Road that borders John Campbell's Meadow.[12] That is it. Still, that meadow indicates John Campbell was living nearby. He was a part of the North River community even though his farm was on the land of the Middle River (near where the two branches of the river merged). What happened to John and his children?

The answer perhaps comes in a court order of February 15, 1748. On that day Daniel Stover of the North River community was given guardianship of all three surviving children of John Campbell who died the year before. The children, Mary, John, and James were all born in the North River region.[13]

It fits. The reason that John Campbell was not on any legal documents was because both he and his wife were dead. His children grew up in another home.

This John Campbell was not considered by earlier researchers, perhaps because he died so young and shows up on only one public record beyond his land patent. The popular assumption of the marriage of John into the Walker family seems most unlikely even as modern descendants of the three orphaned children try to make connection to the Campbells of South Augusta. It does not fit. Most likely, they belong to the John Campbell who was brother of Charles and Hugh of the North River, who came with the family in 1740 and died in 1747.

Access to public record has caused us to take a hard look at the basic assumptions of family history held now for nearly two centuries. Modern access to public records, the ability to travel to primary resource centers, and the probing of genealogical resources far beyond what our ancestors imagined gives birth to

17

a new telling of the story of the Campbells of the North River. In fact, such clarification only builds upon the spirit of the 1911 history and the words of Charles of Ironton, "…the earliest family records often transmit to us that which may be of value, and can not be irreverently ignored, yet it does not command our implicit confidence."

Some day, the same will be said for this text.

CHAPTER THREE

BUT WHO WERE THEY?

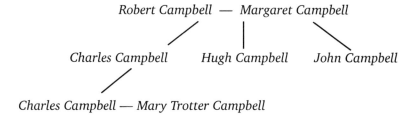

Robert Campbell and probably wife Margaret, though possibly his daughter (see endnote),[1] joined sons John, Hugh, and Charles as they immigrated to America. Most likely they all came together in 1740. Then again, Robert and Margaret may have followed once the three sons had established themselves in Virginia. Robert and Margaret did not have land of their own until 1752.[2] Hugh came with wife Esther and daughter Sarah.[3] Charles and wife Mary came with their sons Robert, Hugh, and John. We do not know if Robert's son John was married in Ireland or was married upon arrival in Virginia. We do not know the name of John's wife. Soon after arriving in America, John's three children were born and shortly thereafter his wife died and then John himself died.[4]

That is how the American story begins of the Campbells of the North River, a list of names in transit. But who were these people? How can we identify them, understand them, and thus appreciate what they passed on?

The answer to such questions begins with the research to determine if the Campbells came alone. Earlier it was suggested that the Campbells were a part of a larger migration of people from a particular region of County Down, Northern Ireland. Such transplanted communities were not uncommon in the colonies. Many were entire church communities led by the pastor of the congregation.

With the help of Ruby Campbell, genealogist of the Clan Campbell Society of North America, a survey was made of the origin of the families of Augusta County. The settlers on Beverley Manor, which comprised most of the county, proved to be a general mix of people from Northern Ireland. There was no concentration of people transplanted from a certain Ulster locale.

That is not the case on the North River. Even as there was a general mix of people from Northern Ireland, and later Germany, there seems as well to be a concentration of people from County Down in the Long Glade and Naked Creek region of the North River community. More particular, they came from a region of a triangle of three Presbyterian churches in the Ulster settlements of Drumore, Drumbo, and Downpatrick. Most likely, the Campbells were a part of this transplanted community. They probably already knew many of their new American neighbors.[5]

What does that mean? Was this simply a response to the advertisement of a ship company looking for people of a certain region to migrate to the colonies? That happened. Most likely, however, any such communal uprooting was born of a shared bond as a community of faith.

If that was true, if this bond was so strong, why did not these very earliest settlers from County Down form their own church in the North River community in the 1740s? Why did they journey to the Old Stone Church?

Eventually there was a Presbyterian church on the North River at Mossy Creek but not in the beginning. At first it was the Old Stone Church and it drew from all directions and united all directions. Church was more than worship; it was a social and political center, a means of necessary news, and even for a time, fortification for a large region of Augusta County. The Old Stone Church was where new people became accepted and sometimes disputes were resolved.

What is puzzling is not that the Campbells journeyed from the North River to the Old Stone Church but why brother Charles didn't join. Hugh Campbell and family were members of the Old Stone Church and tradition says that brother Charles attended church regularly—but didn't join. Maybe it was an oversight. Perhaps Charles and Mary were a part of the forming of an early church at Piney Springs on the North River that came and went.[6] Then again, perhaps the lack of membership gives us a clue to the man who didn't join. To understand why this matters, we go back to the appraisal of belongings of Charles mentioned in the last chapter.

The appraisal states Charles left behind nine books.[7] Those books are key to the times. Those books are the man who owned them. There was the Bible, the Westminster Confession and a volume of Tennant's Sermons and Grey's Sermons, referring to Rev. Gilbert Tennant and Rev. Andrew Grey. Both of these clergy were a voice in what was known as "The Great Awakening."

The Great Awakening began in Europe but it found its force in America. It was tailor-made for people seeking freedom and individual expression. It was the second step of the Reformation. The Reformation began with the transferring of authority and discernment from the clergy to the laity. It was the church "Session" that became the center of the Presbyterian decision making including the scrutiny of clergy and laity alike. Church trials were commonplace.

In The Great Awakening a new spirit arose that the ultimate authority for discernment of human affairs and divine revelation was found in the individual. The individual must be accountable for salvation, knowing the moment when he or she was convicted of sin and transformed by God's grace. It was the individual that determined whether a given clergy was speaking the true word of God, and individuals began taking it upon themselves to let the clergy know it if the clergy weren't authentic to God's word. The Great Awakening was a threat and headache to many clergy. Next, it was the individual that must determine the presence and working of the Holy Spirit in their lives. The Spirit working and its joy became the assurance of God's blessing and redemption. It was a hopeful spirit that salvation was open to more than the previously determined "elect." The Great Awakening was a time of "enthusiasm."

The Great Awakening was also a time of divided worship. There was the necessary gathering of the saints for worship at the church. There was also the gathering of believers in the home. "New Lighters" (people of the Great Awakening) gathered at homes to read and reflect on the scriptures, the *Westminster Book of Confession*, and to read aloud and discuss books of sermons of New Lighters such as Gilbert Tennant and Andrew Grey. When tensions with clergy became too great, the worship in the home became an acceptable alternative, even as it fueled the rise of the Baptist Church and its basic premise of the freedom and witness of the individual.

The finding of volumes of Tennant's and Grey's sermons in Charles Campbell's appraisement, suggests the family was New Lighters. It was a footnote to the work of Charles Campbell of Ironton that pushed the issue further. According to the history of 1911, immigrant Charles Campbell took his family to The Natural Bridge to hear the great preacher George Whitfield, the greatest New Light preacher of his day. It was at The Natural Bridge that George Whitfield baptized three of Charles and Mary Campbell's children in 1754.[8]

That the Campbells would wait to have their children baptized and then make the long, long journey to The Natural Bridge to hear a preacher is a matter of serious question. People

But Who Were They?

didn't make trips of sixty miles with families to hear a preacher in 1754, at least not most. Certainly we have as much reason to wonder of the authenticity of this oral-tradition story as we have questioned the others.

Rev. George Whitfield was on his fifth preaching tour of the American colonies through most of 1754. That tour included Virginia. Perhaps it included The Natural Bridge and perhaps the Campbells journeyed to The Natural Bridge just to hear his witness. Then again, maybe not. Historian C.E. May notes that one did not have to go to Rockbridge County to find the wonder of a natural bridge. The rock formations of the North River of Augusta County created them locally. "In a cavernous limestone region such as North River Basin, sinks and natural bridges formed by the roofs of caverns falling in are often seen. At Mount Solon, a natural bridge spans the headwaters of Mossey Creek. This bridge was used by the Chesapeake and Western railroad until the section of this line from Bridgewater to Stokesville was discontinued some years ago."[9] Perhaps George Whitfield preached at a natural bridge in the North River community.

All of this leaves us with a lot of "perhaps" and not much conclusion. Still, weighing the possibilities of sixty miles or six miles to hear the leading New Light preacher of their day, speaks not just to the Campbell's New Light persuasion, but their devotion. They had not only made the journey, they had waited until then to have their children baptized.

The final clue to the family's spiritual orientation was found by accident, the most awesome find in thirty years of research. There was a day's free time in attending a meeting in Kentucky. Just for fun a trip was made across the river to the Cincinnati Historical Society. There, in a file on this Campbell family, was the personal spiritual diary of William Campbell, son of immigrant Charles Campbell. The spiritual journal bears the date 1786 and is an assortment of excerpts from scripture, prayers, and the Westminster Confession.[10] This was not a published volume, a religious tract made for public consumption. This was a handwritten journal of a believer, recording what was most important to him to remember along with the practical matters of keeping record of the sale of cider.

William was not just a follower. He was a pilgrim, sifting scripture and selected writings of the church that spoke to him along with a reference in the journal to Phillip Doddridge, another outspoken New Light preacher of his day.

To weigh the energies of the New Light movement in the Great Awakening of the 1700s is to discern the general spirit of the times that carried in its wake the Charles Campbell family.

BIOGRAPHY BY LEDGER

We revisit the mention that Charles Campbell died with two sets of cloth clothing. He also had, however meager, a set of china and a walnut table to put them on. He owned slaves and kept at least one indentured servant named William Bishop.[11] Charles not only could read but kept and read books of some literary merit. Again it is a matter of comparing not degrees of wealth but degrees of poverty and if so, such comparisons matter very little.

Maybe we should take a second look. Those distinctions may have mattered. Harsh frontier realities may have leveled the playing field of social status but not entirely. This is underlined in C.E. May's book *Life under Four Flags in the North River Basin*. In fact, May uses the Campbell brothers to prove the point of social stratification in Augusta County life in the 1700s:

> *Besides economic and political factors, the importance placed on family and family name tended to emphasize classes or the stratification of society in Augusta County as well as the rest of the colony.......*

But Who Were They?

The daughters were bequeathed sums of money, a horse, perhaps, and a negro slave woman. For example. Hugh Campbell, a settler on the North River, directed in his will dated March 19, 1771, that his land be divided equally among his three sons: William, Hugh and Charles. He bequeathed his son Robert sixteen pounds and willed his two daughters, Esther and Martha, two fifteenths each of his "movables." By preventing close contacts of daughters of large land owners with members of the "lower classes" of the opposite sex and thus limiting their association to members of their own class, the custom of chaperonage helped develop and maintain stratification of Augusta County society.

The right of husbands to control the actions and property of their wives and of fathers to make important decisions for their children also tended to produce stratification in Colonial society. When a daughter married, control of her property passed from the hands of her father to the hands of her husband. If her husband predeceased her, she was willed what he chose to give her, commonly maintenance for the remainder of her life. The property designated for her maintenance reverted to their children at her remarriage or death. Charles Campbell, who died on the North River in 1775 [actually 1778], left his wife Mary forty pounds, one third of his land, one half of his dwelling house, a riding horse and saddle, two cows, one half of his household goods and a negro named Hit [possibly Kit] for her use during the remainder of her life or until she was remarried. At her death or remarriage, the movable property left to her was to be divided equally among all of his children except William who was devised of all his land, and also a negro boy named Peter, four head of horses, six cows, six sheep, six hogs and a bed [with] its furniture besides.[12]

May's portrait of social stratification needs to be weighed in the spirit and values of the place and time. That social hierarchy existed on the frontier is once again a matter of comparison. It does not equate with the elitism on the Virginia coast among its first families. This was the frontier and whatever divided people was secondary to the bond of survival. This was brought home by the great-grandson of immigrant Charles Campbell. This great-grandson, another Charles Campbell, the "first historian of Virginia," was referring not only to settlers of the Shenandoah Valley in general but his own remembered heritage when he wrote in his history of Virginia:

> *An austere, thoughtful race, they constituted a manly, virtuous population. Their remote situation seemed to them religious freedom, but little interrupted by the ruling powers. Of the stern school of Calvin and Knox, so much derided for their Puritanical tenets, they were more distinguished for their simplicity and integrity, their religious education, and their uniform attendance on the exercises and ordinances of religion, than for the graceful and courteous manners which lend a charm to the intercourse of a more aristocratic society. Trained in a severe discipline, they expressed less than they felt; and keeping their feeling under habitual restraint, they could call forth exertions equal to whatever exigencies might arise. In the wilderness they devoted themselves to agriculture, domestic pursuits and the arts of peace; they were content to live at home….. The gay and fashionable amusements of Eastern Virginia were unknown to them.*[13]

So what is the bottom line when it comes to matters of wealth and privilege? We weigh the comment of the last chapter that Augusta County had "no rich planters… all petty planters, one step above their slaves" with the consideration of social stratification. Were they indeed simple, austere Calvinists or wealthy indulgent plantation owners? Were their lives noble, larger than life as his grandson remembered or was Charles and Hugh Campbell simply more conspicuous of those who made a go of it?

Perhaps the answer is all of the above. Life on the frontier was such an unfolding mix of values and conditions that one could see and measure life from a variety of perspectives. This point was made by Robert D. Mitchell in his work *Commercialism and Frontier: Perspectives on the Early Shenandoah Valley.*

Mitchell notes the misconception by many that the upper Shenandoah Valley was "frontier" during the entire 18th century. In fact, the extreme frontier pioneer life was over in a generation as Staunton emerged from a spot on the road to a true crossroads town. By the 1760s the second wave of pioneers were arriving, those who wanted land that had been broken, improved and promising for commerce. It took a short amount of time for the region to be "settled" or begin to be settled. When one looked closely they found as much settling as they chose to see including significant numbers of literate, ambitious, civic, and commerce-minded folk mixed with those who had no land, were passing through and making do.[14] One saw in it all what one chose to see just as it would be for the frontier-edge societies all through the nation's history.

In the emergence of a settled society and economy, there were those who stayed around, transformed, and stabilized. Hugh and Charles Campbell were a part of that. They arrived to stake their claim in a society of buckskin, elementary farming, hunting, and gathering. They lived the risk of just-opened frontier land. They lived long enough to die with a walnut table, a blue tailored coat and a tea cup and saucer. They had lived and helped nurture the unfolding of that initial transformation.

In the end, the picture of the condition of the first American generations of Campbells, the Campbells of the North River, may not be so much what they had, but in what they gave away—gave to their children. Whatever else life might have been in hardship, risk, and accumulation, each Campbell son was secure in the inheritance of enough land to live his own dream. Each son had enough land to sell to secure the adventure of the call to move west or south or north. Some Campbells did remain in the region into the next century but most, like son William, took the promise and investment of Virginia and used it as security to join a new exodus of an expanding nation.

That investment of affording their children a better opportunity to move on may be the bottom line of the true prosperity of the North River.

BIOGRAPHY BY REVOLUTION

It comes from a letter written over a hundred years after the fact. It is a family story and may bear all the romantic exaggeration of the nineteenth century. Still, it is worth considering that when word reached the North River community that the Declaration of Independence had been signed, at least some of the farmers gathered atop what was called Dickey Hill, later Gratten Hill, and now Wise Hill. They gathered on its peak and lit a bonfire in celebration of liberty. In fact, for a while the story goes, the mount was called Independence Hill.

It was in weighing possibilities against imagination that a conversation was held with the last of a generation of the Wise family that now owned the hill. It wasn't certain if it was used for celebration at the beginning of the Revolution. It was, however, used ninety years later to signal with fire the advance of the Union troops during the Civil War. There is an inscription atop the hill that witnesses to this purpose.

Certainly the hill is the defining landmark of the south side of the North River. After talking with the Wise family elder, I stopped on the way back to my lodging at Staunton to gaze at the hill. I could not keep from imagining the possibility of Campbell

But Who Were They?

Wise Hill, Grattens Hill, Dickey's Hill and ....perhaps Independence Hill in the distance as it is seen from the Robert and Charles Campbell farms

Photo by Nancy Sorells

ancestors gathering in firelight atop the hill to welcome liberty and the birth of a new nation. With that I reread the account of what the Hunter Family of Naked Creek said happened over two hundred years ago.

> *Dickey's hill is the great hill of the Hill Country of Judea. It is on the Augusta and Rockingham County line about a mile and a half from where I was raised. It was called after the revolution, Independence Hill and sometimes, Bonfire Hill. At that day every foot of land in the hill Country of Judea was owned by the sturdy Scotch-Irish, and they loved this country so isolated, so far away from the roar of the sea and oppression, and when the news of the signing of the Declaration of Independence came to this out-of-the-way place, the Scotch Irish of the hill country of Judea assembled and went to this hill. At that time it was pine clad..... and those sturdy Scotch-Irish nation builders, young and old, men and women and children of the whole*

country turned out, and they gathered all the pine knots they could find on this old hill and carried them to the summit and set fire to them, and such another fire has never been seen in that country, and such shouting and cries for liberty.[15]

Perhaps it happened this way. At least this is how the great-grandchildren of the settlers chose to honor the most defining landmark of the region.

What we do know of the family's inclination to revolution was that two months *before* the Declaration of Independence was signed, immigrant Charles Campbell's son, Captain Charles Campbell, a trustee of Augusta Academy cast his vote to have the name changed to Liberty Hall, now Washington and Lee University.[16]

Information on five of the older Campbell sons is sketchy at best and thus we know nothing of their service during the Revolutionary War. We do know of the service of Charles and Mary's fourth son just mentioned, Captain Charles Campbell.

Captain Campbell received his commission from the Governor of Virginia on July 7, 1778. The preceding year his company was a part of the column of 700 soldiers who engaged the enemy at Point Pleasant. At one point he served under General Alexander Hamilton. His company eventually joined General Wilheimburg at Deep Run Church near Richmond. In *The Ripley Bee*, May 16, 1906, the great-grandchildren of Captain Charles Campbell were still recounting their ancestor's most glorious moment of storming General Cornwallis' fortress the night before Cornwallis surrendered to General Washington.

Charles Campbell of Ironton remembered his great-uncle in these words handed on to him:

He was noted for his piety and was fond of books, encouraged literary institutions, and trained his numerous sons and daughters in sound learning. He lived to the age of 85 dying in Rockbridge County where for five years he held the office of High Sheriff. He was as mentioned a Trustee of Augusta Academy and served as a member of the Virginia House of Delegates six years after the Revolution.[17]

Lieutenant James David Campbell of the Alaska Air National Guard, great-great-great-great-great-grandson standing at the grave of his patriot ancestor, William Campbell

We also know that Charles' brother William was in the Revolutionary War and served as a private. William was in the Augusta County militia for at least the year 1782. For his contribution to the war, William was given a land warrant in Ohio that becomes the focus of a future chapter. His tombstone is now graced with an additional marker designating his role in the Revolution.

Mary Trotter Campbell

This work to this point has been mostly a portrait about Campbell men. We have little option. Men were dominant. They were the primary agents of property. They managed affairs and passed their legacy on to their sons. We know little of Campbell women. Robert Campbell, father of Hugh, Charles, and John leaves behind a deed, a will, a property assessment. We know only that his wife's name was Margaret and she signed with an X. We have no idea whether they had daughters, save perhaps one by the name of Margaret.

Son Charles marries Mary Trotter. It is interesting that after two and a half centuries genealogies still refer to her not as Mary Campbell but Mary Trotter Campbell. This one remnant of her own life was clue enough to connect her to James Trotter of Augusta County. James was her brother. It is thought that two of her children married Trotter cousins.

The Campbell immigration to the new world was the Campbell-Trotter migration (James Trotter following to America after 1744) among others of the County Down community that reemerge on the North River. Tracing genealogical information of James Trotter, we found that the family was from Downpatrick in County Down. There was just enough information from the American side to tie Mary and James to the larger family picture of John and Jane Wilson Trotter of Downpatrick. It is a family history that connects Mary Trotter Campbell to the prominent Ruthvan family.[18]

That is all we know of Mary Trotter Campbell, wife of Charles. By the values of her day, mindful that the fulfillment of her life was in her children, we consider her legacy as it unfolded in the generations to follow. Mary had ten children: Robert, Hugh, John, Charles, James, Joseph, William, Elizabeth, Mary, and Sarah. Of these ten children we know of only two lines in depth, Charles and William. Considering the children, grandchildren and great-grandchildren of just these two lines, we find the following: three judges (including one U.S. Federal judge), one doctor, one university president, six newspaper editors, two clergy, the first and second historians of Virginia, a U.S. Congressman, and four state legislators. Go one more generation and one finds the founders of two towns (one in Ohio and one in Illinois), one of the very first pioneer women doctors in Ohio who was an early outspoken advocate of women's rights, and an equally important sister in education, the first woman to sit on the Board of Education in Cincinnati.

This again is only a fraction of the estate Mary Trotter Campbell left behind. To such a legacy we note, again, that at least two, if not more, of her sons were given to the cause of the American Revolution. If the legacy of her children was the measure of her accomplishment, Mary Trotter Campbell was a prosperous woman.

The Land

It is a deeply moving experience to walk the lands where one's ancestors walked. To see the hills and to feel the earth and know it was once theirs to call home is a valued key to knowing who they were.

Where exactly the Campbells lived on the North River in the first four years of their settlement is open to speculation. They may well have lived on the same lands they eventually bought and validated when Augusta County was able to record deeds and surveys in 1745. The North River region was a land open for grabs between two huge land patents, Lord Fairfax's

Home Forgotten

patent to the north and Beverley Manor to the south. Settlers chose land of the North River community that was there "for the taking," so long as the one who took it submitted a survey. Such may well have been the circumstance with the Campbells.

The piece of land that Charles Campbell chose was in a strategic location not far from brother Hugh's. The land was

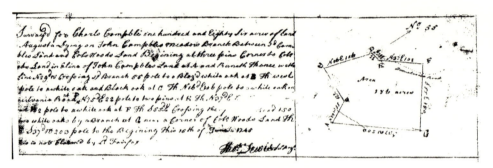

The first recorded lands of Charles Campbell in 1745

intersected by the Pennsylvania Road, which was the travel artery through the colonies. At the same time this land was near to the river and its commerce.

The next year, 1746, Charles buys fifty acres from the crown. In 1747, Charles buys four hundred acres (actually three hundred seventy-six acres) of prime farm from John Anderson to the west of Gratten Hill (Wise Hill) and north of a junction known as Centerville. This became the "home place."

In 1752 Charles buys from the crown a second parcel of land to the east side of Wise Hill on Goodes Creek. That same year Charles' father, Robert, buys two hundred twenty acres of land just west of the home place. In 1760, Robert sells the land to his son Charles, most likely remaining on it until Robert dies in 1768.

Thus, by 1760 Charles and his sons are farming (or farming and renting out) 1,236 acres.

But Who Were They?

Brother Hugh Campbell, who frequently writes his name "Camble," acquired 986 acres in three parcels of land in 1746. Hugh later buys an additional four hundred acres from Charles' brother-in-law, James Trotter. As mentioned before, between the two brothers they own 2,624 acres between Naked Creek and Long Glade Creek.

* * * * * * * * *

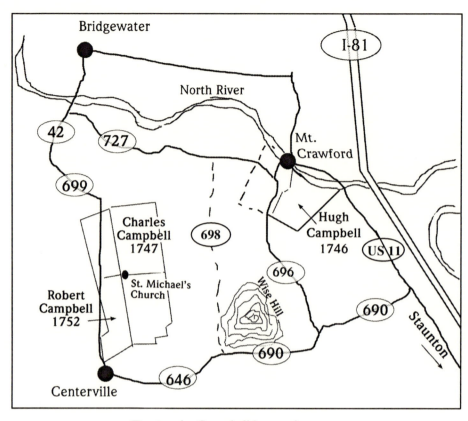

Touring the Campbell home places

It is one thing to see a map, another to savor the view. To that end, the reader is invited to tour the land of the Campbells of the North River that begins ten miles north of Staunton and two miles southeast of Bridgewater, Virgina. Heading north on U.S. Highway 11 from Staunton, one comes to Augusta County Road 690. Turn left on 690 and follow it west until it turns into Road 646 that comes to a junction called Centerville. Turn north of Centerville and less than one fourth of a mile on Route 699 you travel on what once was the farmland of Robert Campbell, our earliest generation Campbell.

Looking north across the farmlands of Robert and Margaret Campbell just beyond Centerville on Route 699

Photo by Nancy Sorrells

Follow that road until you reach the turn off to St. Michael's Church. The turnoff is on Robert Campbell's land. St. Michael's Church itself is on Charles Campbell's land.

St. Michael's Church on Charles Campbell's land

Photo by Nancy Sorrells

The Charles Campbell home place

Photo by Nancy Sorrells

Just beside the church is a road that leads back to the east farther onto the home place of Charles and Mary Trotter Campbell purchased in 1747.

Returning back to Road 699, turn right continuing north as it joins Road 42. Turn right at the junction of Road 42 and Road 727. Follow Road 727 and just past the intersection of 698 one passes the fifty acres purchased by Charles Campbell from King George II.

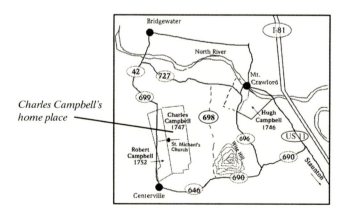

But Who Were They?

Hugh Campbell's plantation looking west from U.S. Highway 11
Photo by Nancy Sorrells

At the intersection of Road 727 and 696, one is on the north edge of the plantation of Hugh Campbell whose land extended east along the river to what is U.S. Highway 11.

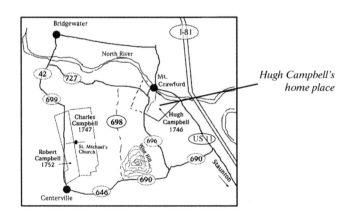

CHAPTER FOUR
WILLIAM AND ELIZABETH WILSON CAMPBELL

Charles and Mary Trotter Campbell
Robert, John, Charles, James, Joseph,
Mary, Sarah, Elizabeth, **William**

ONE LINE AMONG MANY

For the story of the Campbells of the North River to be complete it would need to include the generations that follow all three brothers, John, Hugh, and Charles. That would be twenty children, perhaps two hundred grandchildren. The scope of such a legacy would warrant a small library. It will take the rest of this book just to tell of one family line. Perhaps, in time, other family lines will be lifted up and at least some of the family currents that lead from the North River to the present will be told, a story not only of family but an important part of the unfolding of a nation. From what has been seen in the preparation of this text, other volumes of other family members would be as rich and as involving as what follows.

What does follow is the life of William Campbell, the youngest of seven sons of immigrant Charles Campbell. It is a story that begins by first noting who William Campbell is not.

PROBLEMS

In 1960 Imogene Benson Emory published her family pedigree that showed her a descendant from five Revolutionary War patriots.[1] One of those pedigrees was of Revolutionary Soldier William Campbell. Emory's research connects William and Elizabeth Wilson Campbell as the parents of James Campbell. This is true, but not the James Campbell of her line that married Elizabeth Kerr and extended to Kirkpatrick lines.

It sometimes takes longer to disprove a genealogical connection than to prove one. In this case, it took over a year of intense working with genealogist Patricia Donaldson of Georgetown, Ohio, to prove that the Emory leap of faith was not founded. Such research did not stop with Patricia Donaldson. It also included working with Don McNeil, a genealogist of Emory's line, who was keenly aware of the issues. Finally, the error was discerned by all parties concerned.[2] Unfortunately, such recognition of twenty years ago has not stopped the error from replicating itself and continues on like a bad computer virus that won't go away.

Other considerations include the blending of the families of the Charles Campbell of the North River of Augusta County with the Charles Campbell of south Augusta County. General William Campbell of the south Campbells was confused with—and the descendants mixed with—private William Campbell of the North River. In like manner, some sources state immigrant father and mother, Robert and Margaret Campbell of the North River as belonging to the Campbells of south Augusta County. They are not. Some resources state that all of the Charles Campbell children of the North River were born at Fisherville and baptized at the Tinking Springs Church. This is a good ten miles from the Charles Campbell home on the North River. The North River Campbell children claimed their home address as Miller's Iron Works off the North River.

Ordinarily, such genealogical ponderings are the passing concern for a footnote and do not interrupt the text. In this case, the Emory mistake continues to multiply with new resources confusing the relationship of the Campbells of the North River to the Kerr and Kirkpatrick families. The same is true for the mixing of descendants of the North and South Campbells of Augusta County. The confusion distracts not only from who the descendants are of the two William Campbells but also confuses the flow of both stories.

We proceed mindful of these common discrepancies, in hopes that this volume will not only tell the story of William Campbell of the North River and his descendants but will also help contribute to the dialogue in discerning the early Campbells of Augusta County.

WILLIAM OF THE NORTH RIVER

William Campbell, as noted earlier, was baptized in 1754—suggesting that as the year of his birth. Some sources give the day of his birth as September 1, 1754. Still, the burial records of William at the Red Oak Church in Brown County, Ohio, state that William died July 22, 1822, at the age of seventy-one. This would place his date of birth as 1751.[3]

William's oldest brother was fifteen to eighteen years old by the time of William's birth. Thus by the time William was in his mid-teens some of his brothers not only were on their own but had families, ambitions and were receiving their piece of the plantation pie, a pie some felt was not divided evenly. Charles Campbell died in 1778, the same year that his oldest son Robert died. The year was not over before the grandchildren of Charles were in chancery court, challenging the estate settlement of their grandfather. In this court proceeding filed November 19, 1778, we also learn that brother James Campbell was also dead. Other records show that brother Joseph Campbell was still living in Augusta County and brother John Campbell had moved on to North Carolina.

One thing was accepted. Youngest brother William inherited the last piece of the family plantation and with it the care of his mother until she died. William was twenty-one years old in 1775 and had just married seventeen-year-old Elizabeth Wilson, the eleventh child of James and Rebecca Wilson.[4] William and Elizabeth would begin to have their own family in that same year with the birth of son James W. Campbell, followed by brother Charles who came into the world a year before his grandfather of the same name died. As death gave way to new life, so did peace give way to war.

In 1782 Elizabeth, now twenty-four with four children of her own and a mother-in-law to care for, was in charge of a household with her husband away fighting in the Revolution. To be sure, she had the added help of two slaves and extended family but the tension of the time invites the imagination of how all made do as the Revolution worked its way to resolution. Though we know William served in 1782, he most likely served two other years to qualify for the land warrant he received.

The American Revolution was over in 1783. It was just beginning in the Campbell home. Cousin Robert Campbell, son of immigrant Uncle Hugh, was caught up in "Kentucky fever." All that open land, all that game, all that freedom of a wilderness waiting for settlement. The war was over and lots of people were moving west. Robert was going and he wanted cousin William to join him.[5] Of course, there was mother. Nothing would happen until after she departed this world.

Mary Trotter Campbell died in 1788. In 1789 the Campbell farm was up for sale and sold to German settler John Wise, who was buying up much of the region. The farm sold for three pounds sterling an acre which was top price for 1789. Six hundred pounds was a good grubstake for moving on to Kentucky.

There was, however, a problem, a big problem. Wife Elizabeth by all appearances would not sign away her dowager rights to the Campbell farm. Elizabeth was holding firm and John Wise was waiting for his new farm. A whole year went by and Elizabeth would not budge. Finally, John Wise had no alternative than to take the Campbells to Court. The judge of Augusta County sent a representative to the Campbell home to determine Elizabeth's intent free of the presence of her husband. The court order for September 17, 1790 read:

> *Whereas the said Elizabeth cannot conveniently travel to the court of our said county to make her acknowledgement thereof, I therefore command you that you do personally go to the said Elizabeth and examine her privately and apart from the said William her husband, whether she doth the same freely and voluntarily without his persuasion or threats, and whether she is willing the same to be recorded.*

Elizabeth finally signed the deed, and William and Elizabeth made preparations for the long trek to Kentucky in the spring of 1791. Being a part of the larger migration to Kentucky in this year had particular meaning in the broader story of the history of the just named United States of America. According to David H. Fisher and James C. Kelly in their work *Bound Away*, it was not until this time that the word "west" became place as well as direction. Only as a new nation is formed does the backcountry of the British Empire become "the West" as place and the "out West" spirit of a new nation.

Fischer and Kelly further note that the earliest recorded coinage of the term "frontier settlement," was made the same year William Campbell sold the farm to move to Kentucky. In the next thirty years a whole new lexicon of migration would emerge from this exodus to the West. "Trailblazer," "Pioneer" (in the western sense), the verb "to move" in the migratory sense, were all born out of the spirit of a new nation defining itself by westward destinations instead of European origins.[6]

Also significant in the move of William and Elizabeth Campbell in 1791 is that 1791 marked a change in the intensity and nature of the migration to Kentucky. More and more there was a growing number of commercially-minded merchants and developers. 1791 marked the second and more "genteel" generation of Kentucky settlers.[7] It also elevated the threat of the loss of hunting grounds to native peoples. Chief Tecumseh's raids were at their peak in 1792 as more and more migrants headed down the Ohio River and then the Maysville Road. In the assaults on the settlers of the early 1790s, the alliance of Tecumseh with the British was sowing the seeds of what would become the War of 1812.

It is possible, but most unlikely, that the Campbells joined others of Augusta County that migrated to Kentucky by the Wilderness Road. Most of the settlers of Northern Kentucky that settled along the Mayville Road to the Blue Licks region migrated by means of the Ohio River. They would have left Augusta County north on the Pennsylvania Road to the cut-off to the Old Military Road or Forbes Road as it was called in the 1790s. This road would take them northwest as far as the rivers that fed the Ohio. There they would find timber to build their rafts and float from the tributaries to the Ohio and then southwest to Kentucky. Others who could afford it continued on the road to Pittsburgh where they could purchase a raft and a hire a guide. This northwestern route meant the chance to pick up provisions not otherwise available. They were also provisions purchased at a premium as migrating families were easy prey to merchants with a captive market.[8]

Weeks of travel north and then on the river would eventually lead to the landing at what was then known as Limestone that became Maysville, Kentucky. Again, the migrants were met by merchants providing supplies at exorbitant rates needed for the last ten to fifty miles of the journey down the Maysville Road. Once supplies were procured, the steep arduous ascent began up the bluff of Limestone that would finally give way to the bounty of the sprawling Kentucky lands to the south and the beginning of the Old Buffalo Trace.

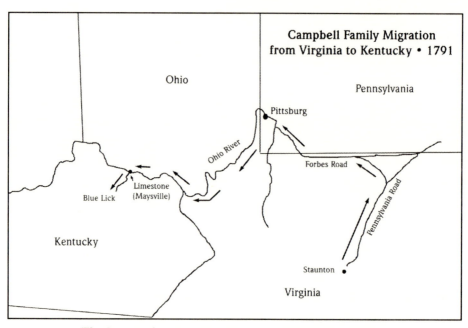

The Journey from Augusta County to Blue Licks, Kentucky

The Landing at Limestone (Maysville)
courtesy Mason County Historical Society

The significance of the settling at the Blue Licks region was noted by Craig Thompson Friend in his work, *Along The Maysville Road.* Blue Licks was the sacred ground of the last battle of the American Revolution. It was the crossroads of a variety of paths, traces, that came together at this place known for its mineral springs. The mineral springs were a natural draw for wild game and thus it was the best hunting spot of the region. It also produced a primitive industry in salt production. The Blue Licks had access to the main branch of the Licking River, which at certain times of the year gave a means of commercial transportation. Still, for all of its possibilities, Blue Licks was also in general a rocky, difficult land to cultivate.

It was also in those early years a frightening land. Craig Friend mentions the region as a place of supernatural wonder, apparitions, horrific rumors and the anxiety that came with the night as sounds nurtured fears of brutal attacks by indigenous tribes.[9] At the same time, for much the same reason, the new Kentucky lands around the Blue Licks lent themselves to heroes that were larger than life defining the meaning of masculinity, including Daniel Boone, Simon Kenton,[10] and as we shall see, a frontiersman named David Duncan.

HARD TIMES

For whatever land William Campbell was able to buy, whatever raw resources were there for the taking, whatever additional freedom the new frontier afforded, the bottom line of Kentucky was one word: poverty. The Kentucky years were hard times. If the Campbells knew any measure of prosperity in Virginia, it was lost in the adventure of the West. We know this first hand from the *Biographical Sketches with other Literary Remains of the Late John W. Campbell* (John was William and Elizabeth's third son):

> He [John] was about nine years old when his father removed to Bourbon County, Kentucky. Being in very

limited circumstances, and having a numerous family, Mr. Campbell was not able to give his sons more than the imperfect rudiments of such an education as could, at that early day, be acquired at a common country school. Indeed, his necessities required the labor of his sons on the farm, as soon as they were able.

John W. Campbell not being, in early life, of robust frame; and being liable to a pain in his head, which was greatly increased by labor in the open fields, it was soon found that he was not well fitted for the laborious occupation of a farmer. And in addition to this, from his earliest years he manifested a strong predilection for the attainment of knowledge.

Some years after the settlement of Mr. Campbell in Kentucky, his brother-in-law, the Rev. Mr. Wilson, of Virginia, being on a visit to the family, and seeing in his nephew an uncommon thirst for knowledge, and thinking favorably of his capacity, proposed to his parents to take him to Virginia, and give him, with his own son, a collegiate education. At this proposal John was greatly delighted, and already looked upon his uncle as his great benefactor and friend. But when his uncle departed, he was not permitted to accompany him. This was a great disappointment to his ardent hopes and flattering prospects. No reason is known for the failure of this arrangement, unless it was the unwillingness of a most affectionate mother to part with her son.

Not finding any prospect of mental improvement while he remained on the farm, and feeling deeply the late disappointment, he in the company of a youth of the same neighborhood, and about the same age, left the services of his father, and traveled to Cincinnati, which at that time was an inconsiderable village. Here they both agreed to learn the trade of a house carpenter, and made an arrangement to this effect with a master workman.

They both were industrious and soon secured the confidence and good feelings of their employer. In the course of a few months, the fathers of both the lads came to Cincinnati in pursuit of them; and finding they were doing well, on the urgent solicitation of their employer, consented that they should remain. But on his return to his family, Mr. Campbell found his wife so much distressed at the absence of her son, that he was obliged to send for him. Seeing the effect which his absence had had upon his afflicted mother; John made ample atonement by an unfeigned sorrow for the pain he had given her.

His parents finding his thirst for knowledge was in no degree diminished, concluded to send him to a Latin school, taught by the Rev. J.P. Campbell, a Presbyterian clergyman. While at this school, and living in the family of his teacher, his parents removed to Ohio, desiring that their son should follow them as soon as his engagements at the school should be expired; which he accordingly did.

He afterwards studied Latin a short time under the direction of the Rev. Dunlevy, in Ohio. This school was five miles from Mr. Campbell's; but the distance was walked most cheerfully, morning and evening, by this ardent youth, who considered this an important step to the attainment of his cherished hopes. He was afterwards sent to prosecute his studies under the Rev. Robert Finley, in Highland County, in the same state. This gentleman established the first classical school in Kentucky, at which several of the most distinguished men of that state were educated.

> *His father not being able to raise the means of purchasing books, or paying for his tuition, John was compelled to resort to manual labor as his only resource. He worked morning and evening in clearing ground, and in this way paid his expenses. And such was his ambition and capacity, that the time spent in labor was made up by increased application, so that his progress was equal to that of any member of his class.[11]*

This excerpt from the life of John W. Campbell provides the following insights into the Campbell family as a whole:

1. The Promised Land of Kentucky was a hard bargain.
2. Listen to Momma.
3. There had to be more than this.

John W. Campbell took great pride in telling of his plight of overcoming the adversity of his family's poverty in Kentucky. It was for him a badge of honor and it gave him reason to return home and to share in delight the fields he once cleared as a youth. He lived the American "can-do" spirit and became a living symbol of rags to riches. For him, the poverty of his youth was a virtue, the crucible of character.

Not everyone in the family wore their poverty quite as well. Younger brother Joseph N. Campbell, who also aspired to offices of public service, found the limited means of his youth not just a badge of honor but a matter of humiliation. As he ran for the Ohio State Legislature, a letter from the opposition was read in the *Georgetown Castigator* of September 4, 1827:

> *As a man of integrity Mr. Campbell is looked upon with an eye of distrust; that there is sufficient cause for doubting his purity of principle I shall by and by have occasion to show; but if he even possessed integrity in a high degree, is this the only ingredient we wish in the character of a statesman? As to Mr. Campbells literary*

achievements, they will scarcely bear to be put in competition with those of any other candidate whose name has yet appeared on the representative list; his education, like my own, was unhappily neglected when young, instead of going to school at the proper age, he was set to watching wolves and making wind-mills. His claim to talents stands on shallow ground, for in this respect he is considered far below the mediocrity of mankind.

TO MOVE AGAIN

William Campbell was among the earlier settlers to cross the Ohio River into Ohio Military Lands. It meant a journey of perhaps twenty miles to Maysville, then eight miles downriver to what is now Ripley, Ohio, and then five miles northwest on Logan's Trace over the bluff to the one hundred acres of William's new land bounty (eventually it would become one hundred thirty-eight acres). The Campbell's new home was a log cabin near the headwaters of a small creek that would bear the name "Campbell's Run."

Whatever the hassles in uprooting, it was time. The Campbells were ready to move on. Ohio meant not only a reward for William's service in the Revolution, it also meant an end to slavery. Something had happened in Kentucky. A former slave owner had now become not only an abolitionist but one determined to live on slave-free soil. [12]

When the Campbells moved on to Ohio, they did not look back, at least son John did not, not for twenty-five years. When he did return he noted not only the nostalgia of the scenes of his youth but also how progress had all but erased the evidence that that Campbells had once lived there.

I have just returned from a most interesting visit. It was one to the neighborhood in which I spent eight years of my life, counting from nine to seventeen; and this, too, after an absence of twenty-four years. When approaching the limits of my youthful walks, I felt emotions which language is too barren to describe. My thoughts were never less at my command; and strange as it may appear, my heart palpitated at my confusion. The road conducting me to the spot on which my parents had resided, was but little altered in its direction. The course was quite familiar, but the distance much shortened by fields recently cleared. What was called a mile thirty years since, seemed to me not more than half a mile. On reaching a place at which I witnessed my mother in the most frightful danger, by a fall from a horse, twenty-seven years ago, I was constrained to halt. The circumstances of her situation was brought fresh to my memory, and I felt nearly the same degree of horror, anxiety and concern, with which I was then disturbed. As I approached the old improvement, the angle of a field which I had helped to clear, caught my eye. Near this place stood a noble plum tree, which, in the period of its bearing, yielded me fruit. It was not at first discovered; but, upon advancing, it was seen like a skeleton amidst the woods. The cabins which once afforded shelter were gone, and not a vestige to be seen. A new mansion was reared elsewhere.[13]

The migration of the Campbells to Ohio included all the children except the oldest son James W. Campbell who stayed behind to manage his own farm in Fleming County, just north and east of the family homestead at Blue Licks. James remained in Kentucky for an additional twenty-six years, completing the family's migration to Ohio in 1825, three years after his father's death.

Years later, James' son, John Milton Campbell, made a stop near the old Kentucky home on his way to Africa as a missionary. His thoughts bore a sadness not only for the condition of the neighbor children he grew up with but the reminder of the "affliction" of the family they had to endure in the Maysville area.[14] Rev. John does not say what that affliction was. His older brother Hiram does mention years later that the family moved to Ohio out of abolitionist sentiment. Perhaps the two concerns were related.

What is evident is that the dream of Kentucky was not a dream fulfilled. Sometimes expectations do not gel. What is good fortune for one family is disappointment for another. Sometimes, as well, a time of disappointment particularly inspires the desire to make the most of the next move. William and Elizabeth not only made the Ohio move seeking a new beginning, they were bringing grown or nearly-grown children, and soon-to-be grandchildren seeking their own way and fortune.

Ohio would not disappoint them.

CHAPTER 5

OHIO

When the Campbells migrated from Augusta County, Virginia, to Northern Kentucky, they were among neighbors. It may have been a strange land, but a strange land with connections. The repetition of Kentucky place names from Augusta County, Virginia, still bears witness to this movement. When the Ohio Military Lands opened, the Campbells were drawn to the settlement called Staunton, named for the county seat of Augusta County, Virginia. Later its name was changed to Ripley. Today Ripley is just upriver from Augusta, Kentucky, named for Augusta County, Virginia.

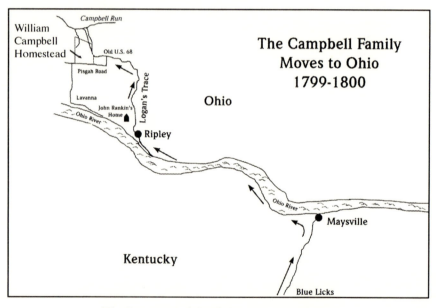

The Location of the William Campbell Farm

The Campbells of the North River at Ripley were among others of the Shenandoah, and that connection was not only security and fellowship but it kept communication open back to the land from which they came. Later generations would move west not only born of opportunity but connections to family who had gone before. When the Lilley family of Augusta County moved to Brown County, Ohio, in the 1830s it was to relocate near "Uncle Campbell." When Congressman John Campbell ran against Allen Trimble for Governor of Ohio, it was an awkward battle of good friends and confidants. It was also a relationship that went back to Augusta County, Virginia, where both were born along the headwaters of the Shenandoah.

The land that William Campbell claimed was his warrant for the Revolution. It corners on what is now old Highway 68, a few miles north of Ripley.

It was in walking the approximate region of the homestead in the early 1980s that I came upon a lifelong resident of the region. He remembered that down along the creek there was an old log cabin that stood until the early 1900s. "That might have been it," he said. The name of the creek was "Campbell's Run."

Pointing Down to Campbell's Run and Farm

And what was life like for the Campbells in Ohio? About the same as Kentucky. Judge W. W. Gilliand, whose father was one of the earliest pastors of the Red Oak Presbyterian Church the Campbells attended, wrote in the *Ripley Bee* of September, 1898:

> *The people were nearly all poor—many of them living in log cabins in the small clearings they had made in the forest. They had no carpets on their floors, very little and very cheap furniture in their homes, and most of their clothing was made with their own hands. I have attended prayer meetings in the old school house near my father's and the "brilliant" light we had was from two or three tallow candles stuck in tin candle sticks.*

> *I do not think I ever saw a carriage at Red Oak, before 1832, except one belonging to John W. Campbell, judge of the U.S. Court [Son of William and Elizabeth] and a two wheel affair my father owned called a "sulky." The older people and the younger too, who could afford it, rode on horse back; and oftentimes man, wife and child were on the same horse. Many of the young men and women walked to church, one, two, three or four miles, carrying their fine shoes and stockings in a bundle until near the church, and then sat down on a log and put them on. This is not hearsay of record but what I have seen oftentimes.*[1]

The early records of the Campbells in Ohio are sparse. There is the 1805 deed to the farm. There is also in the famous Draper Papers a record of the baptism of William and Elizabeth's daughter Fidelia on March 22, 1803.[2] The baptism took place at the home of Edward Evans as the White Oak Church at that time was a home church. A few years later the White Oak Church became a part of the Red Oak Presbyterian Church. There is the record of the marriage license of Caldwell

Tweed to daughter Polly (Mary) Campbell in February, 1813 which reminds us that the Campbells did not move to Brown County, Ohio, but the part of Clermont County that later became Brown County.

As mentioned, William and Elizabeth moved to Ohio with grown or nearly-grown children. This must have meant great help in establishing the homestead. It also meant that the children were soon to make lives of their own. One son, Joseph N. Campbell, became manager of a general mercantile store in Ripley. The ledger of Campbell Mercantile can be found at the Cincinnati Historical Society. That ledger showed a running account for Joseph's parents. Unlike other customers, there were few references to items purchased, just the amounts. When William died in 1822, his son cleared the account at his own expense.

At the same time we are mindful that daughter Elizabeth married William Humphreys. William Humphreys also owned a general mercantile store in Ripley. We do not know if William and Elizabeth had a running account at the Humphreys' store but it does suggest a certain discernment that William and Elizabeth must have had when they went shopping in their small town.

In 1831 son Samuel S. Campbell became the third mayor of Ripley, and on October 1, 1832, Samuel officially set the beginning corner of Ripley from which all existing and future lands and buildings, public and private, would be surveyed.[3]

The previously mentioned son Joseph was not only a store owner but became a regional circuit judge. A family civic spirit was emerging, led by son John W. who was determined to have an education whatever the cost. In 1809 John W. Campbell became a representative to the Ohio State Legislature and then in 1815 he was elected to the first of five terms to the U.S. House of Representatives. We will examine more of this in the

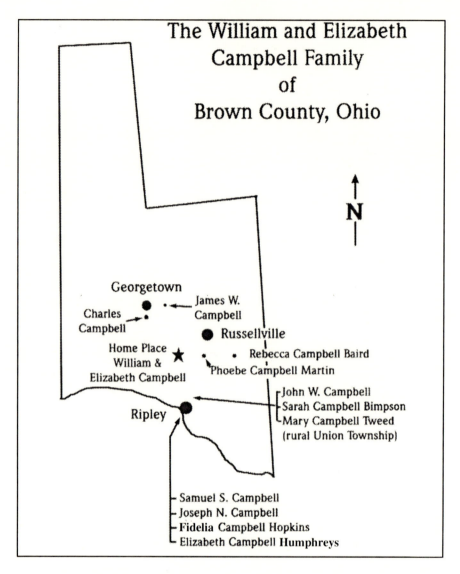

chapters that follow but for now there is the recognition that the Campbells had found their niche in the frontier and were collectively participating in the emergence of a settled and developing new land.

William and Elizabeth did have their moments as they approached their later years. This should be the golden age that bears nobility, and no doubt it did, but with exception. Few moments of thirty years of research were so amusing as the discovery in 1984 of the Red Oak Presbyterian Church session minutes. These minutes record the church trial of William Campbell on the charge of public drunkenness on the occasion of his own logrolling. This author confirms that as he read the church record he could distinctly feel the rumble of the earth as Grandfather William rolled over and over in his grave.

The Red Oak Presbyterian Church Records read as follows:

> *Red Oak. June 3, 1812: Whereas William Campbell is by common fame charged with having been intoxicated at his own logrolling on the 19th of March last, the Session agreed to take up the charge and inquire into the truth of the report as soon as convenient. Ordered that Mr. Martin cite Mr. Campbell to appear at our next meeting and answer to the above charge and that Mr. Salisbury cite as a witness John McConnaughy and Samuel Tweed.*

> *Red Oak, June 13, 1812: William Campbell having been cited agreeably to ye order of our last appeared and said that on the day of his logrolling he drank some burnt whiskey as medicine for a complaint which he had. That he took some in his coffee. That he drank some with a waggoner who was passing along the road and that he drank grog in ye clearing, he didn't remember how often but he said he did not think he was groggy, or at least not much and was not sorry for anything he had done but was sorry he had given any offense. The charge not being fully acknowledged the session proceeded to examine witnesses.*

> *John McConnaughy being sworn said that he was at Mr. Campbell's logrolling last spring. He did not remember that he saw Mr. Campbell drink any liquor*

that day. But his gestures were uncommon and such led him to think he was intoxicated. Those gestures he said he could not otherwise describe than by saying he appeared more loving than common.

Sam Tweed did not appear. The case of Mr Campbell was therefore deferred until our next meeting and Mr. Salisbury was ordered to cite Mr. Tweed again.

Red Oak. August 14, 1812. Mr. Campbell's case continues. Samuel Tweed being duly sworn said that he was at Mr. Campbell's logrolling last spring. That he saw Mr. Campbell drink some liquor and that from his long and intimate acquaintance with him he thought him more disposed to laugh and talk than he would have been if he had not been somewhat intoxicated. That some others of ye company appeared to be of ye same opinion on that day. But that he heard him say no bad words nor did he see him act improperly.

The session after mature deliberation on ye case of Mr. Campbell judged that ye charge against him was supported and that he should be rebuked for his improper use of spirituous liquor and admonished to be more circumspect in the future, which was done.

William Campbell lived until 1822, dying at the age of seventy-one. Elizabeth would live another ten years. Together they twice challenged the growing edge of the frontier. John W. Campbell, a U.S. federal judge at the time of his mother's passing mentioned, "How desirable that all parents should confer such privileges upon their offspring."[4] The comment is interesting mindful that the "privileges" they bestowed were born not out of land as the generation before but the character of the family enduring together.

Still, for all that William and Elizabeth lived to see in their children, it was all but a preface to the even more profound influence of their grandchildren and great-grandchildren as Ohio made its way towards development, industrialization, and the Civil War.

The chapters that follow are not a complete picture. They follow primarily the legacy of the Campbell sons and their children. Such is the availability of the record.

*The Red Oak Presbyterian Church,
home church of the William and Elizabeth Campbell family*

CHAPTER SIX
JOHN W. CAMPBELL

William Campbell   Elizabeth Wilson Campbell
James, Charles, **John W.** *, Joseph N., Elizabeth,*
Mary, Rebecca, Samuel, Phoebe, Sarah, Fidelia

In review, William and Elizabeth had sixteen children. Five died in infancy. The eleven children who grew to adulthood were James W., Charles, John W., Joseph N., Elizabeth, Mary, Rebecca, Samuel, Phoebe, Sarah and Fidelia. Of the eleven surviving children all but James W. Campbell moved with William and Elizabeth across the Ohio River. James W. and family moved to Ohio twenty-six years later.

As mentioned, by the time William and Elizabeth were in their sixties their children had become married and productive members of the Ripley and Red Oak churches and the Ripley and Russellville communities. It beckons imagination to consider family gatherings and with that the family gossip, family politics and shared family ventures in commerce. One especially wonders of such gatherings when brother John W. Campbell came home from Washington City, now Washington D. C., with first-hand information of the business of the nation.

Brother John W. managed, as a youth, to squeeze from the meager resources of the frontier a classical education in Latin and Greek. With that he also received what he wanted years before as a youth but mother would not allow, an education back in Virginia. This time it was not Uncle James Wilson sending him to school, it was studying with Uncle Thomas Wilson as an apprentice to the law.[1]

John W. Campbell

In 1808 John W. Campbell received his license to practice law and was admitted to the bar in Ohio to become the prosecuting attorney for Adams and Highland Counties. In 1809 he was elected to the Ohio legislature.[2]

In 1811 he married Eleanor Doak of Augusta County, Virginia. Shortly thereafter John W. Campbell was a part of the Ohio regiment in what became the War of 1812. John W. was a quartermaster serving under Allen Trimble. As quartermaster his role was behind the lines providing supplies and the general care of the soldiers. Still, more than a supply captain, John W. was a barometer of the troops. Discontent was building out of rumors promoted by a hired scout with mixed loyalties. One of Trimble's subordinates was seriously considering mutiny. It was John W. who kept Trimble informed of the building malaise, and when it came to a head it was Trimble, along with the John W., who talked the troops into holding the course. The arrival of General William Henry Harrison finally convinced the regiment to press on into confrontation with the British.

Looking back, Colonel Allen Trimble remarked, "This incident enabled me to judge of the material at my command. John W. Campbell, afterwards a member of Congress and judge of the U.S. Court, who acted as quartermaster, told me the next day on our march, whom I might depend upon in an emergency, and I soon found that he had formed a very correct and reliable judgment."[3]

These words of Allen Trimble are an important index into the character and talents of John W. Campbell. John W's manner of mingling, observing and then quietly influencing the situation without calling attention to himself unless forced to do so became his hallmark in both the legislatures of Ohio and the U.S. Congress. He was a moderate's moderate. "He was not an intense partisan by nature and his speeches indicated the equanimity of his disposition."[4] Or as another commentary

*Early portrait of Congressman John W. Campbell.
The first likeness of any Campbell family member.*

put it, "his political principle was not given to extreme."[5] With a keen sense of process and compromise, he was the glue or grease in getting things done. Seldom was he heard in debate, but he was often the go-between on legislation of the Ohio House and Senate. He understood procedure. At such a vulnerable and volatile time in U.S. history there was a particular need for people like John Campbell in tending the whole of the legislature. John Campbell was once third in the voting for Speaker of the U.S. House of Representatives. If John Campbell had continued to serve in the U.S. Congress, it was widely held that he would have become the Speaker.[6]

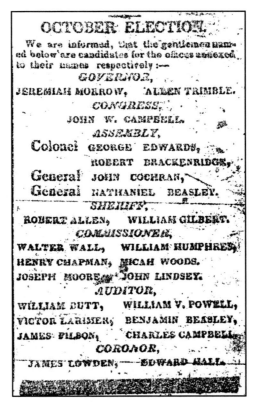

Advertisement for John W. Campbell for Congress

The road to the U.S. Congress took four years. He was first considered in 1812 when an additional house seat was given to Ohio. He was not well-enough known in the state at the time. In 1814 United State Senator Thomas Washington resigned to become Governor of Ohio. John Campbell was third in the running to fill the empty Senate seat, "...an indication of the place he was becoming to have in state politics. In the fall of 1816 John Campbell was elected to the U.S. Congress by a large majority, and reflected by the people of his district by an almost unanimous vote five times, until he, against their strong and reiterated remonstrances, declined being a candidate."[7]

If John himself was not disposed to debating, his life in the U.S. Congress gave him access to some of the great debates and orators of his day. John Campbell was a great observer. In the middle of the debate of April 2, 1824, between Henry Clay and Daniel Webster, John Campbell wrote to Governor Allen Trimble: "We are yet on the tariff. Mr. Clay made an able speech of six hours. Webster is making his now. I think he is not as eloquent as he was on the bank question."[8]

On another occasion he wrote to Governor Trimble of the rough and ready life of Washington politics. This was especially true during the years 1825, 1826, and 1827 when John Campbell "lamented the party violence which prevailed, and still more the baleful consequences that were likely to flow from it."[9] In the letter John Campbell wrote of a duel between John Randolph and Henry Clay:

> *On Saturday evening at ½ after four, Mr. Clay and Mr. Randolph fought a duel. They stood at the distance of 30 feet. The first fire being harmless, they took their positions a second time. Mr. C. fired his ball paper [wadding] through Mr. Randolph's clothes. Mr. R. having discharged into the air, extended his hand which the other cordially received.*
>
> *The friends of Mr. C. were General Jesup and Mr. Johnson of Louisiana and those of Mr. R. were Mr Tatinall and Hamilton. Other gentlemen were present. Mr. C. Challenged, for words which he considered <u>personal</u> used by Mr. R. in a speech in the Senate.*
>
> *This affair will be differently regarded. Some suppose calls of this kind may operate as an abridgement of privilege and freedom of debate. Others think Mr. Clay has a right to put down such bitter enemies in any way he can. The offensive words I understand were "that the president and his secy. [secretary] were insulted as puritans and black legs." Severe enough!*
>
> *Mr. R. has always claimed and exercised in debate a*

design of liberty which would have been denied to any other person. He ought to be called to order though upon the person calling he should make eternal war. Some of the eastern gentlemen say Mr. Clay is <u>down</u> in their country forever and rather wish his removal.[10]

In the same letter John Campbell said of President John Quincy Adams:

It may be supposed by our good people that Mr. Adams is not very religious when they shall have heard that he has purchased a billiard table with public money and retains Mr. Clay.

Over and over again biographies noted John Campbell's character to stay above the muck and mire of this time of extremely bitter confrontation. He was an advocate against the bargaining to get Panama. He stood against nullification, or a state's right to overturn whatever federal law was not in their interest. At the same time, he was not in favor of protecting American businesses through tariffs on overseas goods. He was opposed to slavery even as he was deeply concerned over the growing rift between the North and South. Born of his own struggle for an education, he was a fierce advocate for public common school education, land grant colleges, and public lecture programs or lyceums. He once made a Fourth of July speech advocating that every dollar spent by people to celebrate freedom should be matched by funds they give to provide better libraries to continue that freedom.[11] Finally, John W. was a strong advocate of public works projects to make Ohio more accessible.

In 1822 John W. Campbell was approached as to his advice for the substance of a well-grounded education. The letter dated January 17, 1823, sent from Washington gives an excellent window into John Campbell's own reading and values.

To a Friend:

Some time ago I had the pleasure of reading your letter in which you expressed a desire to have my advice relative to a course of study which would best serve your condition. To comply with a request so reasonable, it would seem proper, that you should indicate the profession for which you wish to qualify yourself. To attain the elevation of the Presbyterian pulpit, the aspirant is required to pass through Greece and Rome, in what is called classic lore, he must at least have a smattering. To be a physician, a less portion of this kind of literature will answer. To be a lawyer dispensed with.

Without knowing what precisely to what object your wishes may be drawn, I will venture to mark out the following course, which if pursued, will qualify you for the discharge of the important duties of a citizen, and prepare you for the study of law.

Read the Life of Franklin. *If you can catch <u>his spirit</u>, the example of industry which he affords, will be easily imitated, and all your studies be pleasing.*

Study English grammar critically. This can be done without declining <u>hic, hace, hoc</u>, and will be found useful in whatsoever department of life, it may be your lot your to be placed.

To be able to write a fair, easy hand and a good composition, will be worthy of your attention. They offer the highest recommendations to lucrative pursuits. To excel in composition, it will be proper that you take the Spectator, *or some such work for a model. In this study, Dr. Blair's lectures will afford you much assistance.*

Read Geography, beginning with that of your own country. Ignorance of this branch of erudition is a great misfortune to a man of public life as it renders him liable to ridicule and contempt and is a great drawback in reading a newspaper or in ordinary conversation of the day where an entire devotion to trifles does not prevail.

Read Marshall's Life of Washington. *The last volume is replete with the most useful information and deserves several readings.*

I should do you great injustice were I not to mention Rollins' Ancient History *and Gibbons'* Rome. *These will answer and edify. You may master a volume a week without prejudice to the interests of your employer.*

Humes's History of England *and his continuation are considered standards and ought to be read with great attention. They combine much military, political, judicial, philosophical and religious information.*

I can not omit Paley's Philosophy. *I account it a first rate work of the kind. I know of no book of the same dimensions in which is condensed so much important matters.*

I believe these books can be found in the Greeneville Library with many others such as Plutarch's Lives (of the Twelve Caesars) *and Dr. Ramsey's works of nearly equal merit.*

In reading history, it is important to recollect facts, such as where and when a battle was fought, who were the chieftains, what number slain, the political consequences, etc. To become well acquainted with the books which I recommend will not require more time than is usually appropriated to Latin and which would tend to the improvement of your mind I imagine a doubt can hardly be entertained.

You are too old to consume two or three years of these studies of dead languages. This length of time, I will observe would not leave you able to construe with ease. At this period of your life your object ought rather to be the acquisition of useful ideas than to store your memory with words.

My opinions on the course you ought to pursue would be very different were you nine or ten years of age with funds at command.

I have prescribed for you in a hurry, but I do not suppose a month's reflection would induce me to make much alteration except in phraseology.

With wishes that you may daily make accessions to your stock of knowledge.

I am your friend,

John W. Campbell[12]

At the end of his fifth term, John W. Campbell chose to leave the Congress and return to his farm in Brown County. This "availability" did not go unnoticed as he was talked into running for governor on the Andrew Jackson ticket against his old friend, confidant, and military superior Allen Trimble. How could John put any effort into running against someone so valued in his life as Allen Trimble?

Well, he didn't.

In Allen Trimble's autobiography,[13] Trimble notes that if the Jackson ticket had made any real effort they would have won. In a letter dated September 27, 1828, to an unknown recipient, John Campbell said he was "indifferent" to the whole affair and

> **JACKSON & REFORM.**
>
> Frequent elections—moderate salaries and rotation in office—freedom of religion—freedom of the press—freedom of the seas.—JEFFERSON.
>
> [The following is the Electoral Ticket, nominated at Georgetown by the Jackson Convention of Brown county, on Friday the 29th of August last. The election will be held on the 14th day of October 1828.]
>
> GOVERNOR,
> JOHN W. CAMPBELL.
> CONGRESS,
> WILLIAM RUSSEL.
> REPRESENTATIVES,
> THOMAS L. HAMER,
> JOHN COCHRAN.
> SHERIFF,
> JAMES LOUDON.
> AUDITOR,
> BENJAMIN EVANS.
> COMMISSIONER,
> WILLIAM LIGGETT.
> CORONER,
> MOSES LAYCOCK.
>
> ———*———
>
> **OHIO CONFERENCE.**
> Stations of the Preachers in the Ohio Annual Conference, for 1828,-9.
> MIAMI DISTRICT.

Political advertisement for John W. Campbell for Governor

considered his extremely close loss to Trimble to be an amazing show of support.

It was not long after the governor's race in Ohio that Andrew Jackson became president. Jackson then appointed John W. Campbell U.S. Judge for the Ohio District. A biographer states:

> *The Senate unanimously confirmed this nomination, and it was accepted. He carried with him to the bench the same unbending integrity and good sense which had marked his public course. His early habits*

of study were never laid aside.......He generally arose at four o'clock in the morning, to engage in some favorite study. Many of his manuscripts were published anonymously in periodicals of the day.... The honorary degree of Doctor of Civil Laws, without his knowledge, was confirmed on him by Augusta College at its commencement of 1831.[14]

In 1833 an epidemic of cholera swept the Columbus region. John Campbell, age 51, died suddenly in its wake. On the arrival of the melancholy intelligence of his decease at Columbus, a great sensation was produced, for he was universally respected....Some hundreds of citizens from Columbus met the funeral cortege near Worthington, and accompanied the remains of their lamented neighbor to his last home.[15]

This chapter now comes full circle as we try once again to imagine what it was like when John Campbell came home to Brown County to visit both his own farming operation, his many friends, and his considerable extended family.

Reading John's letters from Washington, one tries to imagine the same stories being shared with his mother Elizabeth and father William in their primitive log cabin on Campbell's Run. One also wonders at the example Uncle John made on the next generation, especially a nephew who bore the same name, a nephew John that was hoping Uncle John would help him make a stake in the iron industry. Unfortunately, Uncle John died before nephew John would begin his rise as an ironmaster, which becomes for us a part the next chapter of the story.

John W. Campbell

U.S. Federal Judge John W. Campbell

CHAPTER 7

CHARLES CAMPBELL

William Campbell   Elizabeth Wilson Campbell
James, **Charles***, John W. , Joseph N., Elizabeth, Mary, Rebecca, Samuel, Phoebe, Sarah, Fidelia*

We return to the beginning and the first history dictated in 1828. The Charles Campbell who told the story is now the subject of our story, Charles and his wife Elizabeth.

Charles Campbell, brother of John W. and second son of William and Elizabeth Campbell, was born December 21, 1777, (other sources say he was born December 28, 1778) and lived to be ninety-four years old.[1]

Elizabeth Tweed Campbell
Photo courtesy of Briggs-Lawrence County Library, Ironton, Ohio

Charles was fourteen when the family moved from the North River of Virginia to Blue Licks, Kentucky. At twenty-three Charles moved with the family to Brown County, Ohio, and helped his father William break the ground of the new homestead. Four years later Charles married Elizabeth Tweed and took up farming near Georgetown, where he also was a part-time school teacher. Charles and Elizabeth were married for sixty-seven years.[2]

Charles and Elizabeth had five sons, four of whom lived to adulthood: William W., John, James, and Joseph N. H. "Harvey" Campbell. Of note is that three of the four children that lived either addressed themselves by a middle or third name or initials. Thus, William Wilson was often called "W. W.," James M. went by his middle name "Marcellus" even in the 1870 census. Son Joseph N. H. Campbell went by the name of "Harvey," his third given name. Only son John went by his first name.

We do not know the name of the son who died or to what, but are again to be reminded of the tenuous nature of life and medical treatment on the frontier. This fact was driven home further by the illness of son James who "took ill April 4, 1822, of billows fever and rheumatism and was attended by Dr. [Alexander] Campbell and Dr. Buckner. On July 19, 1822, his right leg was amputated…..for treatments, bread and sweet milk, camphorated spirits, whiskey and barks rollers dipped in sugar of lead were used."[3]

Bilious Fever (Billows Fever) was believed caused by too much bile in the system. It was a diagnosis for any number of feverish conditions from pneumonia to typhoid fever. The medication, "barks rollers" was a form of pastry. In this case it was dipped in the crystals formed of vinegar added to lead (sugar of lead) which created a sweet taste. As to how effective these were, added to bread and sweet milk and camphor, is not known. Still, the whiskey probably worked. [4]

The incident that led to the amputation of James' leg would linger in the family's memory as a bad outcome of the ignorance of the attending physician. It was also the circumstance that would forever change the life of son James. With an amputated leg, he would no longer be able to farm. His life's vocation would have to be sedentary and commercial. James became a tailor, at least for a while. Cousin Washington Campbell was complementing farming with work in land appraisement.

James would come to complement his tailoring by a platting land for development.⁵ Such an eye for land measurement and development would come into full play when he would plat and found the town of Morton, Illinois.

One wonders in the relation in the Charles Campbell family between history and vision. This is the family line that particularly honored and recorded the stories of the past, kept diaries, and at the same time was the family that took bold risks to move on to new territory and new ways of life. That time of moving and risks has a date, the summer of 1834. Leaving in the spring, Charles, Elizabeth, and three of their sons continue the Campbell legacy of moving to the frontier's edge. In this case, the frontier was Tazewell County, Illinois. Oldest son William bought land in June of 1834. In July his brother James invested; that same year father Charles did the same.⁶

Joseph N. H. Harvey Campbell, the youngest brother, was only sixteen when they moved. Still, it is he who dwelled on lifelong memories of Ohio, including a younger classmate for a few years in Georgetown by the name of Ulysses S. Grant. It was Harvey who shared his father's aptitude for history, keeping the family story in print, and it was Harvey who lived the family legacy of moving on to new frontiers, leaving for Iowa in 1857.⁷

When the Campbells moved to Tazewell County in 1834, they identified with the town of Washington some fifteen miles away. Other settlements began to emerge. A few miles south was Tremont, southwest was Groveland. Near the same distance and farther on was Pekin. By the 1840s there were settlements forming in the region that could well have become the established community of the area. New London not only had a general store but a brewery. New London demised as Gibbs Brewery moved to Peoria. Then there was Joseph Evans who farmed one mile north of what became Morton. Evans opened a trading post and post office that became known as Evans Corner. The

Evans location was on higher ground, removed from the more swampy land below. Swamp or otherwise, Morton became the center of commerce, It was platted by James M. Campbell, its founder. [8]

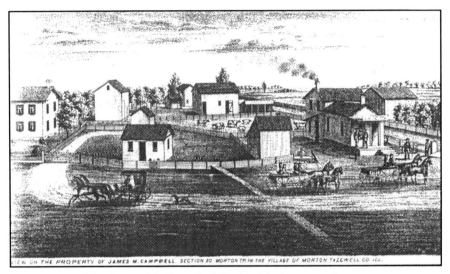

The James M. Campbell farm with the general store that became the center of Morton [9]

James M. Campbell

Eventually the swampy land was drained, thanks to a new emerging local industry of Rapp Brothers Brick and Tile Company. Tiling enabled the draining of some of the richest farmland in the nation. Shortly after Morton was established, it was expanded to three hundred acres. Today, Morton with a population of over 15,000, celebrates its heritage as the pumpkin capital of the world, producing at its Nestle-Libby plant sixty percent of the canned pumpkin in the world. The annual pumpkin festival draws 100,000 people.

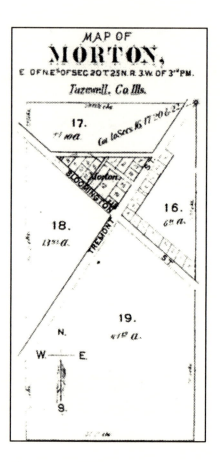

The plat of the town of Morton by James M. Campbell[10]

Morton is also the home of the huge parts distribution plant of the Caterpillar Corporation, handling 375,000 different parts that are sent out around the world. The town is also the headquarters the Morton Building Company that provides metal commercial buildings across the nation. For decades Morton was also home of what became Morton Pottery that produced what are, today, most-valued collectibles.

Now the obvious question: Where did the Campbells come up with the name of Morton? *The Pictorial History of Morton* by Donald and Ruth Roth refers to the early published belief that the Campbells named the settlement for the twice governor of Massachusetts, Marcus Morton. The book wonders if perhaps the Campbells were related to Governor Morton. Another, more sentimental legend rests in the connection of James M. Campbell, a bachelor late into his life, with the Webb family. The Webbs invited Mr. Campbell with some regularity to dinner. James Campbell named the town in tribute to Mrs. Webb. For a bachelor to name the town for another man's wife lacked discernment. So, he named the town according to her maiden name.[11]

The last story bears the chivalry of another day but it also seems a bit of a stretch. Why, then, would the Campbells name the town for the Governor of Massachusetts? No, the Campbells of the North River were not related to Marcus Morton, nor was Elizabeth Tweed Campbell's family that came from Maryland.

A possibility might come from the brother who wasn't there. To understand how Morton became Morton, we might consider the second son that moved not west to Illinois, but east to Hanging Rock, Ohio, and from there to found the town due east of Hanging Rock called Ironton. His name was John C. Campbell. A clue to Morton, Illinois, might be found in Ironton, Ohio.

* * * * * * * * *

The second son of Charles and Elizabeth Campbell, John C. Campbell, was born near Ripley, Ohio, in 1808. Like his brothers, John received a basic rural education. In 1828 at the age of twenty, John gave up farming and went to work for the husband of his aunt, Elizabeth Campbell Humphreys. Uncle William Humpheys, as mentioned earlier, was in the mercantile business in Ripley. With John working with him, William decided to expand his operation and open a second store north of Ripley at Russellville. John managed the expansion of the business. John also realized the slow-paced life at Russellville was not for him.[12]

Uncle Humphreys offered another option. John could take his accumulated six-hundred-dollar savings from working in the store and invest that savings in Uncle Humphreys' steamboat called "The Banner" that worked the Ohio River.[13] Steamboat management was better than a store clerk—but not much. On the second trip of the *Banner* to Pittsburgh, John happened upon a passenger named Robert Hamilton. Robert Hamilton was an ironmaster of the Hanging Rock region at the Pine Grove Furnace in Lawrence County. Business was booming in the iron business. Within a year two new furnaces would open in the Hanging Rock region. John sold his interest in the *Banner* and went to work as a clerk for Andrew Ellison and Robert Hamilton at the Pine Grove Furnace and helped with the iron mill at Hanging Rock. John started as a clerk. Advancement came quickly, not only in his position but partnership in the iron industry.[14]

What was a six-hundred-dollar savings in the country store had grown to a thousand dollars. To that, John offered his first year's wages as additional collateral, taking up lodging where he could find it and making do on next to nothing. John needed more and, as mentioned, was counting on the Campbell family back in Brown County to stand with him, especially uncle John W. Campbell, the now U. S. federal judge, and uncle Joseph N. Campbell, who ran the store in Ripley. If both uncles were open to such investment, such hopes were dashed as both uncles died suddenly within weeks of each other of cholera in the summer and early fall of 1833.[15]

Instead, John turned to his aunt Fidelia Campbell Hopkins and his father Charles Campbell. With support from his family, John invested fifteen hundred dollars towards the building of the Lawrence Furnace not far from Hanging Rock. At Lawrence Furnace, John moved from clerk to superintendent. His continual reinvesting of income and now company profits back into the industry put his name on a new corporation. In 1832-1833 John was an apprentice, learning and making his stake in the iron business. In 1834 John's big break came with the construction of the Mt. Vernon Furnace north of Hanging Rock. Not even three years into the iron business, John joined Andrew Ellison to form *Campbell, Ellison and Company*.

It was in the midst of not only learning the ropes but buying the ropes and then tying the ropes into a conglomerate, that there entered into the drama of iron production of Hanging Rock the presence of a one Joseph Firmstone, who according to the census of 1860, was by occupation a "Gentleman." Joseph G. Firmstone was not just from Shropshire, the iron-producing region of England but was astute at the latest processes of iron production. *The Iron Trade Review*, October 22, 1925, stated, "The first Firmstone, the father of William, came to America from England to build a hot blast stove at the charcoal iron furnace in Sciota County, Ohio, near Portsmouth and this was the first hot blast stove in America."[16]

Well, the stove that was built was near Hanging Rock, not Portsmouth, in Lawrence County, not Scioto, and was built not by Joseph G. Firmstone but his son William, who did shortly follow his father to America. Joseph G., indeed, knew the business and was called to Hanging Rock for the task, but it was his son William that had the ambition, ingenuity, and vision to convert a cold blast furnace to hot. *The Virginia Cavalcade* (Autumn, 1957) states of William, "In his early twenties he managed an English ironworks for two of his uncles. In 1835 he [William] immigrated to America.....he added a hot blast successfully to an Ohio Furnace in 1836, to another in Pennsylvania three years later."[17] One hundred years later William Firmstone would be remembered for "his engineering and managerial genius."[18] It all began in America in Lawrence County, Ohio, with an investment in William Firmstone's father.

William Firmstone

Joseph G. Firmstone was given an opportunity he couldn't refuse: the newly built La Grange Furnace. Iron magnate John F. Gould sold Joseph Firmstone the La Grange Iron Furnace with no money down. Firmstone would pay off the debt for the furnace as he went along. All of this would go sour within nine years.[19] Still, in 1835, the Firmstones carried the day. For the next two years, the frontier iron production facilities at Hanging Rock would be at the forefront of iron manufacturing innovation in America. No sooner was Vesuvius Furnace fitted for hot blast than work was begun to do the same to La Grange Furnace and eventually to others such as Lawrence Furnace.

It is interesting that today in the Ironton area there is no memory of William Firmstone's father or the rest of the family that would live out their lives in Portsmouth, Ohio. What is remembered is that John Campbell helped build the first hot blast iron furnace in America with a man named William Firmstone. The date 1863 is given at the Vesuvius Furnace historical site and park for the inauguration of hot blast iron production. The last two numerals have been mistakenly transposed from 1836. It may also be a matter of opinion as to whether the Vesuvius Furnace was indeed the first hot blast of iron in the country. The Rev. F. W. Geissenhainer of New York claims to have made the first hot blast iron and applied for a patent of his process in 1831. The patent was granted in 1833. [20] Another report suggests that William Firmstone made iron of hot blast in Pennsylvania for a month in 1835 using anthracite coal before he made his way to Hanging Rock, Ohio.[21] Four states claim they are the site of the first hot blast iron in America. Some of that has to do with the meaning of "hot blast." Still, it is the Vesuvius Furnace near Ironton that bears the tradition of being the first hot blast furnace and its remains are a monument to that spirit of early adaptation and invention.

We don't know if John Campbell and William Firmstone ever met after their few years together building furnaces at Hanging Rock. Certainly the opportunity was there when William Firmstone came from Pennsylvania to visit his family in Portsmouth or when he came back to Ohio to cover his father's debts in 1850. Certainly Firmstone and Campbell had to know of each others ongoing work. John Campbell became the most noted ironmaster of his time in Ohio and Firmstone's innovative genius as an ironmaster in Pennsylvania would accumulate a number of "firsts" of continued innovation in the iron industry.

One wonders if Firmstone's spirit might have encouraged John Campbell's own experimentation that led to his own "first" of placing the boilers on the furnace stack in 1841 that ran the steam-driven blowers. [22]

Still, as we shall see, the innovation and vision of John Campbell was broader than the refinement of the iron he produced. He was not just an industrialist. John saw people as more than workers needed to make iron, he saw, as well, the reverse. Industry was a means of developing a vital, enlightened and moral community. More than an ironmaster, John Campbell was central to the inception, the momentum, and realization of what became Ironton.

* * * * * * * * *

While John was quickly working his way into the iron industry, he was also becoming quite literally a member of one of the first families of iron in Ohio, the Ellisons. John Ellison immigrated to America in 1795 and in 1810 opened the Brush Creek Iron Furnace in Adams County, Ohio. One of John Ellison's daughters married Robert Hamilton who, with Andrew Ellison (John's son), brought the family operation to Hanging Rock. In 1837, while the great experiment of the hot blast was underway, John Campbell married Elizabeth Caldwell Clarke, the niece of Robert Hamilton and the cousin of Andrew Ellison. They were married in the Hamilton home in Pine Grove.[23]

As John Campbell was becoming a part of the Ellison family circle, he was also opening the door for other members of his own family to join him.

Just as John was making his mark at the Mt. Vernon Furnace, he took two months off to be with his family near Georgetown, Ohio. Perhaps some of this visit was to finish up family business of those who left for Illinois the year before. Beyond that, however, John made the first of many offerings to the extended Campbell family to come and live in Lawrence County. That first invitation was to John's cousin Hiram. Living across the Ohio River in Kentucky, Hiram Campbell had found his own way into the iron industry. In 1835 John talked Hiram into clerking the Mt. Vernon Furnace in which John was investing. It would also give Hiram his own access to bigger and better things in the wake of all the many other opportunities that "Campbell and Ellison Company" might afford.

This early connection between these two cousins is sometimes overlooked. The cousins had teamed together for nearly fifteen years before John invited Hiram into what was only their latest shared business venture of forming the town of Ironton.

Hiram was more than a clerk at Mt. Vernon. Hiram was very much a part of some of John's growing array of projects, including a little-referenced iron foundry and outlet called "Campbell and Ellison of Cincinnati." The person in charge of the Cincinnati "house," as iron operations were called, was a man by the name of David T. Woodrow.

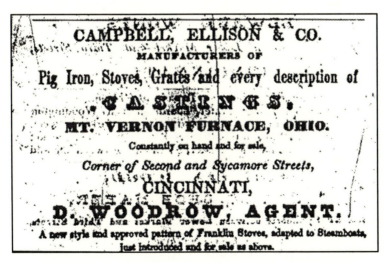

Advertisement of Campbell, Ellison & Company of Cincinnati. The location of the Cincinnati iron shop is now the playing field of the modern Cincinnati Red Sox baseball stadium.

By the late 1840s the Cincinnati iron shop was not producing as well as might be expected. Thus, John Campbell sent his cousin Hiram to evaluate and instruct the situation. In a letter dated November 25, 1848, D.T. Woodrow wrote to John Campbell of Hiram's visit and he was not happy. Woodrow acknowledged that iron sales were not what was expected and there may indeed be need to sell out, but sell out in due course and in the right way. Still, Woodrow added that is no reason to send Hiram to address him in such an abrupt and rude manner:

> *Hiram talked and acted so shamefully while here that I could not understand him. Everything was grumble, grumble with him....he said you were very dissatisfied about the foundry and intimated all were so until I told him I would sell it as soon as I could take advantage. He [Hiram] thought all the other furnaces were making more money than our concern....Everyway he grumbled at me and my management. Then just as he was going away he thought the best way would be to make no change and indeed went on talking just the contrary from what he had said the day before. He said if he were here and had the management of this house he would do it....he would come to Cincinnati to live and he knows he has not the capacity to take charge of this house.*

The letter continues with the following observation of the relation between the two Campbell cousins:

> *He [Hiram] said you [John] were complaining about him all the time and for my part I have no doubt but you have good reason and suppose he wants to shift everything that's wrong on me.*[24]

This letter stands in want of a rebuttal from Hiram. There are probably many sides to what happened regarding the Cincinnati foundry. What we do have is the record that both

David T. Woodrow and Hiram Campbell were worthy business associates. Both of these men were leaders in their own right and would go on to make substantial business contributions under the umbrella of the larger iron empire of John Campbell.

In the tiff of the moment, in the struggles to nurture industry, we sense how much John Campbell was early on the bottom line. We are mindful of the effort Hiram made to own up to his commitment and how much he lived in the light of his cousin's expectations. We note that whatever happened between D.T. Woodrow and Hiram in that moment was resolved. At least they would work together on several projects in the next ten years. Besides, Woodrow was the cousin of Hiram Campbell's wife, Sarah Woodrow Campbell. The family connections seem endless. One can't help but wonder how much John Campbell's gift of industry was found in keeping it all together, keeping the peace, including peace in the family.

In 1846 John Campbell left the care of the Mt. Vernon's operation to cousin Hiram and returned to Hanging Rock and its central place in the overall iron industry. John bought the Ellison family home at Hanging Rock from wife Elizabeth's uncle, Robert Hamilton. John was about to make his move for an enlightened metropolis, a noble, moral, glowing light of progress on the river. Hanging Rock was to be that model city. No sooner does John move to Hanging Rock in 1846 than he makes the following pronouncement:

> *We could soon have a town with 10,000 inhabitants here…we could extend one branch of the railroad through the headwaters of Raccoon [river], where there is crib timber, another fork through Ross county to Chillicothe, and so on to Columbus, intersecting with other roads running north…..In this way we could take freight and travel from the Canal, and make Hanging Rock the largest town between Columbus*

and Wheeling—the railroad would cut off all trade from Gallipolis and Portsmouth—then it would have no competition to contend with.....provisions would be come cheap from the interior......It would be far enough from any city to become one of the largest in the West...On our own energy all would depend.... why shouldn't it go on?......Why should we not be the actors in this?....We have the capital....we have the capacity...Why should we not have the energy?[25]

To such passionate vision John Campbell also had a plan. That plan to make Hanging Rock one of the great cities of the West was to begin with a railroad. John Campbell put that plan into motion but it was motion that was quickly squelched. Uncle Robert Hamilton, Elizabeth Campbell's favorite relation, the man who fourteen years before offered John his first job in the iron industry, and five years later opened his home for John's wedding, was not agreeable. It was evident that Robert saw in John's ambition a chance to make a killing on the new railroad that Robert knew John needed to make things happen at Hanging Rock. Any new railroad to Hanging Rock would need Robert's existing railroad. The two men became more distant as the discussions went along. In this case, family bonds did not foster reconciliation. The demise of Hanging Rock and the founding of Ironton became, in part, a sad family matter of power and control.[26]

The building of a railroad town had reached an impasse, at least on the surface. Below the surface, John Campbell quietly took his vision and frustration to others.[27] The scene was set for the now mythic all-night Halloween ride of 1848. Prominent settlers James Willard and John Peters awakened John Campbell the next morning to announce their support of his vision for a new town and railroad just up the river from Hanging Rock. Not long after, the Ohio Iron and Coal Company was formed. It became the agency that would create a new railroad and set into motion a new town east of Hanging Rock. It was the birth of Ironton.[28] Besides the initial support of Willard and Peters, we must mention the importance of Caleb Briggs to John Campbell. Briggs was Ironton's first postmaster.

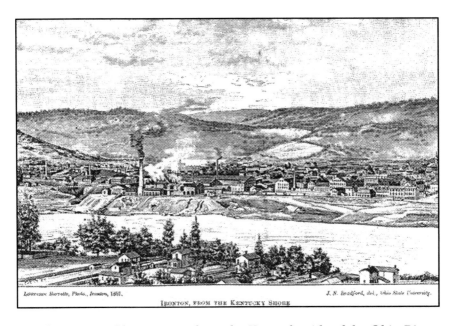

Early Ironton, Ohio, as seen from the Kentucky side of the Ohio River
courtesy Lawrence County Historical Society

Ironton, Ohio, was founded by John Campbell in 1849, one year before his brother James M. Campbell founded Morton, Illinois. The record shows that the growth of Ironton was immediate. "People flocked to the new town, attracted by its moral, as well as its industrial promises."[29] At the center of it all was the man, the mover, the risk taker who was the moving spirit involved in all aspects of the community's growth. John Campbell "provided for churches, [though he himself did not join one], for school houses, for manufacturers, for every healthful influence and industrial advantage. He was then in the prime of life, and he infused his energy to everybody. Every good work he encouraged with money and personal influence.

His good nature and his clear insight of things made him the founder of a new town. He despised shame and delusions, and built only on honest worth and merit."[30]

In April, 1849, John wrote a letter to cousin Hiram Campbell, asking Hiram to join John in founding the new town. It is a letter only recently discovered. A synopsis of pertinent details follow:

> *Dear Cousin,*
>
> *From the* Lawrence County Gazette *sent to you with this, you will see that we are going about a railroad and building a town. I have taken an active part in making all the arrangements and I am still more sanguine of the success and importance of the undertaking the more I reflect on it....*

John then goes on to consider his dreams of a town with all the establishments of civility, all the requirements for industry and the promise of a railroad to connect his town to the world. There were 11,000 lots to be used for every good purpose and John could see those purposes woven together, but he needed help, Hiram's help. John envisions Hiram's ability to invest (especially now that Hiram was in charge of the estate of uncle Samuel Campbell). John encourages Hiram to come with his mother or his cousin, William S. "Smith" Humphreys, to examine the whole operations. John then concludes:

> *I have in view for you and your mother with Smith Humphreys and others to become citizens of this will be town, in a few years. When society is to be formed and the right spirit given to education etc. etc. I can cut out work for thousands but those must be the right kind of people to execute part of the good of the great multitude or it will be neglected.*
>
> *Respectfully your cousin,*
> *John Campbell*[31]

Another such letter still extant in the family is mentioned by Mrs. Marion Blair Edmundson who writes, "I have a letter from John Campbell asking my great-grandfather [who married a daughter of William and Elizabeth Campbell] if he would come up to Lawrence Co, as he, John Campbell was starting a new iron furnace and would like Mr. Humphreys to build some new houses for it. Also regards from cousin Elizabeth to the family. That is how Grandmother got up here from Ripley."[32]

Others that came to Lawrence County included John's Campbell cousins Amanda Doak Humphreys and John Humphreys and cousin Florence Baird, who married a son of Hiram. Aunt Rebecca Campbell Baird's son, Samuel Baird, came to Ironton and became a stockholder in the Ironton nail mill. He also married Mary Jane Steece of Ironton, daughter of one of the founders of the city and colleague of John Campbell. Samuel Baird left Ironton but continued in the iron business and eventually constructed the Baird Iron Furnace in Perry County, Ohio.[33]

Ironton was a whole new chapter of the Campbells of the North River. Until Ironton, the Campbells were agrarian. To be sure, Ironton was not the big city but it was a new life in a fast growing and dynamic town. For the first time a significant part of the extended Campbell family was living off an economy of industry.

One wonders what the social interconnection of these Campbell families were as they left Brown County and formed a new life together in Ironton. One also wonders how such a large extension of the family affected the comings and goings back and forth to Brown County. With that, the consideration of money earned in Ironton that became security to those back home.

A few years later they were building the First Presbyterian Church of Ironton, John Campbell's cousin Hiram provided for the stained-glass windows in honor of his brother John Milton Campbell, missionary to Africa. Such a gesture was not simply a matter of one family's expressed grief and honor. John Milton Campbell may have stopped at Hanging Rock but he had never been in Ironton. He died before there was an Ironton, but there were many in Ironton who knew cousin John Milton Campbell and for whom the loss of his life and the honor of his life was a personal family memory.

On South Sixth Street in Ironton is the beautiful Italian Villa-style home that is now the Lawrence County Historical Society Museum. In 1886 it was the home of Colonel George N. Gray and wife Elizabeth. It was in their home that one of the most famous American Abolitionists died, the Rev. John Rankin. Rev. Rankin was the grandfather of Elizabeth Gray. It is also worth noting that Elizabeth Gray was also the great-granddaughter of William and Elizabeth Campbell. John Campbell was Elizabeth Gray's second cousin.[34]

The graveyard of Olive Furnace where Aunt Sarah Campbell Bimpson is buried

photo: Jan Rader

Outside of Ironton are remnants of the once-vital iron industry. Dotted across the hillsides of Lawrence County are the stacks of the old iron furnaces. On a green slope above Olive Furnace is the graveyard of Sarah Campbell Bimpson, yet another aunt of John Campbell. Sarah Campbell Bimpson was the youngest daughter of William and Elizabeth Campbell. Sarah was widowed at an early age and left to care for two small sons. Her brother, Judge John W. Campbell, bought the Bimpson farm in Brown County to give Sarah money to live on. Sarah remained with her children on the farm, now owned by her brother, until the boys reached young adulthood. At that point, Sarah was invited by nephew John C. Campbell to move to Olive Furnace north of Ironton, and her sons began to work their way into the iron business.[35]

One half of the eleven children born to William and Elizabeth Campbell had one or more offspring that moved to or near Ironton, Ohio, to work in the iron industry.

* * * * * * * * * *

John Campbell continually invested his earnings back into the growth of Ironton. Each new prospect for industry and each new facility to nurture community included John's involvement. John Campbell lived for the well-being of his town.

The fruition of both John Campbell's personal fortune and the town's prosperity found its zenith in the years of the Civil War and the decade that followed. High quality iron was at a premium and there was none better than what came from the Hecla Furnace run by John Campbell. The iron bore strength to rival any in the world. It was used for both the shielding of the Union Navy's first iron-clad ship, the U.S.S. Monitor, as well as the metal used in the forging of the cannon known as the "Swamp Angel." The cannon was used at the battle of Charleston in 1863.

John Campbell's commitment to the war effort was not only in the making of iron. He was also appointed by Abraham Lincoln to supervise the gathering of income tax for the 11th Collection District of Ohio.

By the early 1870s John Campbell's personal fortune had risen to over a million dollars. Ten years later he would lose it all. He was forced into a bankruptcy that demanded he sell everything he had except the home residence. By that time John was too old and the competition too fierce to reclaim his losses in the iron industry. John's son-in-law supervised the public sale of the private fortune of the man who lived for his town.

Henry Howe, writer of Ohio history, met John Campbell six years after John's bankruptcy. Later he commented, "I scarcely met with another of such grand patriarchal presence; of great stature and singular benignancy of expression; he made me think of George Washington."[36]

John Campbell, iron industrialist and founder of Ironton

John and Elizabeth Campbell had seven children of their own.[37] One of those children died in infancy and four of the children were never married. These include Emma, Albert, Clara, and Charles. We make special note of Charles, an engineer, who also became the first real family historian and whose picture graces the first chapter. It is he who is referenced in the first chapters of this book as "Charles of Ironton." He is also the last Charles in the family. This name that was so repetitive for the first four generations suddenly fell out of use.

Son Albert Campbell was a veteran of the Civil War. Daughter Emma was physically immobile and died at an early age. Sister Clara was never married but her romance with coffee magnate Charles Arbuckle and his remiss in fulfilling his promise to marry Clara was the scandal of the day filling gossip columns of New York newspapers. Clara took Arbuckle to court for not fulfilling his formal promise to marry her. She sued for one hundred thousand dollars. She received forty-five thousand.

The two children of John and Elizabeth Campbell who did marry lived lives of public note. Mary J. Campbell married Henry Safford Neal, who served in the Ohio legislature. He then became U.S. Consul to Portugal. He returned to serve in the U.S. Congress and finally was appointed Solicitor General by President Arthur and served as such until President Cleveland took office.

Daughter Martha E. Campbell married William Means, who became the mayor of Cincinnati in 1881. Their daughter Gertrude Means married W. A. Julian, who became U.S. Secretary of the Treasury during the Roosevelt administration.

John Campbell died September 3, 1891, at the age of eighty-three. It was a day of deep mourning in Ironton. His funeral procession was sixty carriages long. With his death was the fading story of iron manufacturing for the region. John's obituary read: "He was an original stockholder in the Ironton rolling mill and Olive foundry and machine shops.....It was through his influence that the first telegraph wire was extended here. He was president of the Great Union Iron Company and proprietor of Hecla Furnace, and for years President of the Iron Railroad Company." To that could be added that he was one of the founders of the Iron Bank [now U.S. Bank]. He built a stove foundry, a factory for the manufacture of an iron beam plow and the Star Nail Mill, one of the largest in the country. John even gave vision to a U.S. Coast Guard station at Ironton that was never realized.

But it was not just his business sense and ambition for which he was remembered. John's obituary continues: "He took an interest in every man who tried to do something for himself. He was a friend of the unfortunate. No wonder the people of color flocked to his funeral and tearfully viewed him for the last time. He was their friend and in the dark days of slavery, no fugitive ever came to this town, searching for freedom, but that Mr. Campbell took his hand, gave him money and sent him on. His home was the asylum for the oppressed of those days."[38]

Just how much John Campbell took interest in others will be underscored in a chapter that follows on the Underground Railroad. For now it is worthy of note that after one hundred fifty years of the founding of Ironton, John Campbell is not just remembered, he is revered. Across the Midwest there are any number of cities and towns who remember that one person or those persons who made it happen and the city was born. On the town's anniversaries the name is mentioned and the old house on the hill where he or she lived is fixed up for the celebration. In truth though, we usually have little memory beyond a name and some monument of who those founding persons really were.

That is not the case with John Campbell. The memory of his vision, compassion, commitment to justice, dignity in misfortune, and his genuine humaneness in all aspects of business and labor are still lauded as an example of civic responsibility and decency. Today, there is a one-man theatrical production of John Campbell and another play produced of the spirit of his wife, Elizabeth Clarke Campbell. Historians continue to rewrite the saga of his life and a furnace festival is held where he is remembered. Campbell street, Campbell School, and the Campbell home in Ironton are tributes to his life.

Still, for all the many ways John Campbell is yet remembered, it is continually in the context of his work, the issues of slavery, and the town that he helped design and name. There is a need to see John Campbell in yet another context; his life as an extension of the family in Brown County from which he came and from which he drew to help make Ironton.

The moral values that were so important to John Campbell were extensions of the values of the larger family that gathered at John Gilliland and John Rankin's churches in Brown County. The abolition spirit of his youth became the abolition passion of his maturity. The values of community service and the building of a community with moral character have roots in the principles of his civic-minded namesake Uncle John Campbell, Congressman and Judge. It was his Campbell family that did invest with John in the iron industry. The shared block in Ironton with the two Campbell homes, John's and Hiram's together, speak not only to shared business interests but to shared family ties.

Today, joyous occasions are remembered of going back to Ironton and visiting the First Presbyterian Church of Ironton. There the ancestors once worship. From there some were laid to rest and in memory of them some of the stained-glass windows were named. It is a sacred place intensified by the greeting of its members, whose kindness gives the deepest meaning to the words "welcome home." Ironton is home. John Campbell made it so. When his own family headed west to help form Morton,

Illinois, John Campbell headed east and brought his family with him that were a part of the formation of Ironton.

* * * * * * * * *

We return to Morton, Illinois, to consider the youngest of the sons of Charles and Elizabeth Campbell, Joseph N. H. Harvey Campbell born January 30, 1816. It was Harvey who, some believed, actually named Morton, Illinois. Joseph N.H. Campbell grew from a child to adulthood in Tazewell County, Illinois. Then in 1857, Joseph took the mantle and moved farther west, settling near the town of Peoria in Mahaska County, Iowa. Joseph became School Board Director and then in 1868 was elected to serve as Representative to the Tenth General Assembly of the Iowa legislature.

Of note is that a distant cousin, Frank T. Campbell, a descendant of William Campbell's older brother Charles, would be Lieutenant Governor of Iowa a few years later. In 1886, Harvey and wife Maria moved to Russellville, Iowa, where he lived out the remainder of his days.

What we know of Joseph or "Harvey" as a person is from the superlatives exclaimed upon his death in what was the largest funeral that anyone could remember. Proud of his country and in times of peril a true patriot, two of his sons serving in the Union Army. "Mr. Campbell was a well known and highly respected citizen…his reputation was that of an honest, upright man, strictly just and generous, and one whose judgment was rarely at fault."[39]

For all such words might suggest, such character was formed out of seemingly constant family tragedy. Joseph Campbell was a man acquainted with grief. Joseph and Maria had twelve children. At the time of his death, only one was surviving and he, Chester, not for very long. Joseph and Maria, with twelve children, had no living grandchildren in their old age.

Joseph N. H. "Harvey" Campbell
Iowa House of Representatives, 1868
used by permission State Historical Society of Iowa

Among the tragic deaths of their children was son Marion, who excelled in the Iowa infantry during the Civil War and was commissioned captain. At the close of the Civil War he married and chose an ill-fated sojourn to settle in Mississippi. He was elected to the Mississippi legislature and then elected to the Mississippi senate. Nonetheless, Marion was a Yankee "carpetbagger" politician who was also an officer in the Union Army. Marion, for whatever his intentions, was not appreciated in the South after the war, especially in Mississippi. His life was constantly harangued by warnings and threats. Then, the yellow fever struck. His wife and children died. Instead of consolation in his grief, Marion was stripped of all his property, taken to the depot and ordered to leave. A few years later he was found drowned in the Skunk River of Iowa.

One half of an obituary of Joseph Campbell's life was given to the details of the loss of this son.[40] Following the death of his wife of sixty-seven years, Joseph's father Charles Campbell left Morton and sons James M. and W.W. to spend his last days in Iowa with his son Joseph. When Charles died in 1871 his body was taken back to Morton, Illinois, for burial at the family plot in the town cemetery. At the funeral were all four sons including brother John from Ironton, Ohio.

Together they honored a father who had lived nearly a century. Charles' life spanned the family's story from the home place in Virginia, to survival on the Kentucky frontier, to the emergence of the family in the center of the mix of politics, economics, industry, and the social expansion of the nation. Charles Campbell was buried in one of the two towns his sons had founded.

*Dr. Allan Campbell standing at the
Charles Campbell family grave marker, Morton, Illinois*

CHAPTER 8
JOSEPH N. CAMPBELL

William Campbell   Elizabeth Wilson Campbell
James, Charles, John W. , **Joseph N.,** *Elizabeth, Mary, Rebecca, Samuel, Phoebe, Sarah, Fidelia*

Thus far, the story of the Campbells of the North River has been mostly about men. Men led, women supported and raised families. Those were the values of the day. Such is the reason this book follows the lives of fathers and sons—until now. If Elizabeth Campbell left a hint of strong will, it was her great-granddaughters, one of whom would bear her name (along with another Elizabeth of a different line), who would define what strong willed, forceful, and visionary character was all about.

This chapter is a tribute to two of the most remarkable women in Ohio. *The Cincinnati Post* lists Edith Campbell as one of its 100 Cincinnatians who made a mark on the 20th century.[1] She was the first woman of Cincinnati to be elected to public office, an election so important that President Taft came from Washington for the sole purpose of casting his ballot for Edith Campbell to serve on the Cincinnati Board of Education.[2] She was the first woman to chair the Board of Trustees of the Ohio State University. Her contributions to vocational education gave call for her to be a part of a White House Task Force On Education. The *Ladies Home Journal* of June 1915 outlined all that Edith Campbell had accomplished, concluding it was "enough to fill a book."[3] Edith was then forty years old, her life and accomplishments not half over. When Edith died in 1962, Cincinnati named its newest school Edith Campbell Junior High.

Edith lived with her sister Dr. Elizabeth Campbell, the first female physician of Cincinnati and a pioneer of national prominence in the promotion of public hygiene and family planning. In February 1943 the American Social Hygiene Association gave six awards to persons they deemed pioneers in American Public Health. The First recipient was John D. Rockefeller Jr. The second was to Dr. Elizabeth Campbell who "was one of the pioneers of women-in-medicine and her outstanding success in her field has blazed the way for the many able women who have followed in her footsteps."[4]

Today the home where the two Campbell sisters lived in Cincinnati is a stop on the walking tour of the city.[5] It is just down the street from the Elizabeth Campbell Women's Health Center.

Still, all of this is a rush to the future. We need to go back to the sisters' beginnings, back to Ripley, Ohio, back to the children and grandchildren of William and Elizabeth Campbell.

* * * * * * * * *

The youngest son of William and Elizabeth Campbell was Joseph, who would live out his life in Ripley, Ohio. Like his older brother Samuel S. Campbell, who at one time was mayor of Ripley, Joseph was inclined to public service, running for the state legislature and serving as an associate judge of the Court of Common Pleas for Clermont County and then later Brown County. "He traveled to Williamsburgh to court for many years, through the wilderness country and through the mud."[6]

It was for Joseph N. Campbell that nephew Joseph N. H. Campbell, of Morton, Illinois, was named. Joseph was the favorite brother of U.S. Federal Judge John W. Campbell and a lengthy tribute to Joseph is included in John's book of literary remains. In that tribute John W. Campbell wrote of his brother: "Joseph N. Campbell was born July 5, 1783. He possessed a mild and peaceful temper, and was remarkable for his morality even from an early age. He carefully avoided the vices so common and so destructive to youth. Mr. Campbell was not favored with a liberal education; but by his own industry he acquired the knowledge suited to his station, and such was calculated to give him respectability and render him useful in society."[7]

This reference to his education gives reminder to a quote in an earlier chapter when Joseph N. Campbell ran for the state legislature. It was in that bid for election that one of his adversaries referred to Joseph's "neglected education" by noting Joseph "set to watching wolves and making windmills."

Joseph's financial security was underwritten by the previously mentioned operation of his Mercantile Store in Ripley.

NEW GOODS,
Joseph N. Campbell,
HAS just received from Philadelphia, and is now opening at his old stand in Ripley, a general assortment of Merchandise, suited to the present and approaching season, and consisting principally of the ollowing articles;
DRY GOODS,
GROCERIES, Queensware, Hardware, Cutlery, Iron, &c. &c. in all their different varieties. He returns thanks to his former numerous customers, for the liberality heretofore extended to him in his line, and now gives a general invitation to all who wish to get good bargains to call and examine his assortment,—quality of his goods, &c. He feels no hesitancy in saying that from the low rate at which his goods were purchased, he is able to sell as cheap as any of his neighbors.
Ripley, June 25, 1832. 2

Joseph N. Campbell's store advertisement in the Georgetown Castigator

In 1816 Joseph Campbell married Elizabeth Kirker, the daughter of Ohio's governor, Thomas Kirker. Joseph's and Elizabeth's children included William B. Campbell who remained in Ripley and was employed as a bookkeeper. It was through Joseph that William B. Campbell inherited the spiritual journal of his grandfather and namesake William Campbell.

Joseph was a vital force in the founding of the Presbyterian Church in Ripley, Ohio, where he was a ruling elder. His support was essential to the church's early financial security as well as the church's vision in supporting missions.[8]

In 1833 a scourge of cholera struck Ripley "and spread terror and death among the inhabitants." One of those stricken was Joseph Campbell. "In the evening preceding his death he felt better health than usual. Early in the morning it was discovered that the cholera had commenced its ravages upon his system. He found himself extremely feeble. He told his wife that he could not recover; expressed his hopes of future happiness, and exhorted her to bring up the children in the fear of the Lord. He soon became too debilitated for conversation and expired in the afternoon on the same day."[9]

The death of Joseph deeply affected his older brother Judge John Campbell. John lost his usual cheerfulness for life. "He was my favorite brother. He was dear to me through life; I mourn over his death."[10] As mentioned, it was only months before John W. Campbell died in Columbus from the same scourge of cholera.

Whether the Ripley home where Joseph N. Campbell lived became the residence of his son William is not known. Son William's residence in Ripley is a historic town landmark, not only for its Federal-style design and age but for the fact that it was here that Joseph N. Campbell's two granddaughters Edith and Elizabeth were born.

Home of William B. and Mary L. Campbell in Ripley, Ohio, birth place of Elizabeth and Edith Campbell.

Elizabeth, mother Mary, brother William L., father William B., and Edith
Photo: Cincinnati Historical Society

William B. Campbell's subdued life as a bookkeeper was the quiet before the storm. William and Mary saw promise in their elder daughter's artistic talents and prepared the way for Elizabeth to become an artist. Secretly, Elizabeth was stealing away to a local Ripley physician's office where she lost herself in medical books. Elizabeth was also drawn in wonder to the treatment of her younger sister Edith's infirmity. Edith was frail and her physical needs warranted a private tutor. Once, while being fitted for a dress, it was noticed that Edith had a deformed hip. Time was not kind to the ailment. Edith needed more than the local doctors could provide.[11]

Eventually, Elizabeth made her intentions known of going to medical school. Her parents were against it. Her friends were against it. No medical school in Ohio would accept her.

So Elizabeth would go to the University of Michigan.

At Michigan Elizabeth would study with Dr. Victor Vaughn, who was an authority in epidemics and advocate for public health. He became an important focusing inspiration to Elizabeth and she took that inspiration back with her to Ohio to finish her education. Women were finally eligible for medical studies in Cincinnati and that was where her degree was granted. Still, for her internship Elizabeth chose once more to leave home. From May until August 1895, she worked the wards at the Prison Hospital for Women at Framingham, Massachusetts.

At the prison Elizabeth's concern for public health grew as she cared for many doing time for prostitution. Wrote Marguerite W. Zapolean in her comprehensive review of the two Campbell sisters, "Elizabeth saw tragedies that a knowledge of social hygiene might have forestalled. She became more than ever determined to prevent as well as cure disease." Zapolean then mentions Elizabeth's return to Ohio, and the big challenge of establishing a medical practice in Cincinnati. Her father writes in his Bible: "Daughter Elizabeth left home this November 14th

'95 for Cincinnati as a Dr. She hopes she will succeed in her profession and may the Lord bless her and take care of her."[12]

Indeed, Elizabeth did succeed and the doors of Christ Hospital were open to her. In a series of articles addressing notable emergency cases, Elizabeth became regarded for what the *Ohio State Medical Journal* referred to as her "unusual ability as a diagnostician."[13]

Dr. Elizabeth Campbell as a young physician
photo: Cincinnati Historical Society

No sooner does Elizabeth become established in Cincinnati than she sends for her family, the whole family, including her sister Edith.

In 1999 *The Cincinnati Post* ran a special article on sister Edith Campbell stating "Edith Campbell, whose decades of tireless and stirring social activism produced a dazzling array of firsts in education, women's rights, and civil rights, was often called Cincinnati's foremost female citizen."[14]

Edith Campbell was born in 1875. As noted, her poor health kept her from attending public schools. She was blessed with fine private tutors in Ripley who fueled her appetite to learn. This led one biographer to write, "As sometimes happens, Edith Campbell was *fortunate*, to enjoy poor health. Missing school certainly contributed to Miss Edith's independence of spirit. Added to this was a voracious appetite for reading and a remarkably retentive memory."[15]

For one year Edith attended Coates College in Terre Haute, Indiana. Not only did she do well in a public education setting, her very proud father was known to have said, "Edith was one of six in her class of ninety to receive highest distinction."[16]

Moving from Terre Haute to Cincinnati, Edith not only finds through her physician sister Elizabeth the road to health but entrance into the University of Cincinnati. There Edith blossoms. She joins so many organizations that she was always seen going to the next meeting.[17] She was vice president of her 1901 graduating class. In 1906 she receives a master's degree in economics from the University of Cincinnati. Upon graduation Edith began to teach economics at the University and more importantly she began to research and teach the economics of working women.

Edith became a local, then regional, and finally national authority on women in the work place and the practical need for vocational training in public education. Today these issues are still with us but they are far from novel. In 1910 they were the edge of education and Edith was a pioneer.

Edith's concern for fairness and opportunity for women in the work force came suddenly into public eye in the shockwave of a tragic accident of the daughter of a prominent Cincinnati family. Betty Van Meter Ames, one of two biographical essayists of Edith's life best states what happened:

> *In 1908, Mr. Jacob Schmidlapp, a wealthy Cincinnati banker, asked Miss Campbell to suggest a suitable memorial to his daughter killed in an accident. He had come to the right person whose practical sense was infused with idealism. She set to work to organize and direct a loan fund to advance money (without interest or any legal obligation for repayment) to young women wishing to complete their education and prepare themselves for a vocation. In connection with administering this fund, Miss Campbell saw the need for an employment bureau for women and girls which she began. Another outgrowth of her association with Mr. Schmidlapp, a result of the combination of his generosity and her creative energy, was the building of model apartments for working women in several Cincinnati suburbs. In all her relationships with the young, Miss Campbell acted as guidance counselor, mother confessor and guardian angel.*[18]

In the wonder of her vision and energy there is one curiosity. Why would Edith Campbell establish an employment bureau for women when there were already such avenues for promoting jobs for women? The answer is that many, if not most, public channels soliciting employment of women were corrupt. Thus we find another cause for Edith and for us a chance to savor the power she brought to words. Edith was a force of persuasion, causing the press to wonder over and over how one of such small and frail stature could command such presence in the company of the few and powerful. She was the first president of the influential Cincinnati Woman's Club which she helped form. In the *Journal of the Academy of Political Science* of New York City in 1910 we find her words that still ring with the passion of her persuasion.

> *No other agency stands so little for efficient service as the employment bureau. Scorned by the scientific because of its unscientific methods; condemned by the honest and conscientious because of its unjust earnings and unscrupulous policies; despised by the employer because of its failure intelligently to meet his needs; ignored by the seeker for work because of its deceptive guarantees, the employment bureau is far from commanding the respect of the industrial world. Consequently, employer and employee usually dispense with its services, and the woman who is busy molding for herself an industrial career gives little thought to so ineffective a method for determining the direction of that career.[19]*

Edith then addresses the issue of the education of women for the work place:

> *That we are still far from adjusting education woman's life is lamentably apparent. The public schools seem averse to training her for a trade lest the unadvisedly throw her into the employer's hands. The plea is still loudly heard that the girl must be trained for home life and for home life alone.....[not long ago] a man of deep mental and spiritual insight said to me, that he considered all legislation for making women's industrial life easier a mistake, because intolerable conditions in the factory and workshop will ultimately force women back into the home. Just where "back into the home" is, no one seems to know! With the industrial processes in which woman has worked from time immemorial taken from the home, the exhortation to stay at home and follow the example of her industrious grandmother seems a bit hard to follow. This fear, however, on the part of educators, this restiveness on the part of especially men concerning*

> *women and the trades, should not be altogether ignored, though part of it is due to plain cowardice in refusing to face things as they are.*

Biographer Betty Van Meter Ames completes the portrait of Edith Campbell with these words, "...a little woman with boundless energy and enthusiasm, of great courage and determination. She was far ahead of her times. She fought with all the organization skill and feminine diplomacy she possessed for human rights, including a richer fuller life for women, children and minority groups."[20]

The following year, 1911, Edith ran for the Cincinnati School Board. In that election she noted, "Nine-tenths of our teachers are women. One-half of our parents are women. One-half of our children will be women."[21] It was time a woman sat on the Board of Education. Upon winning the election and the beginning of the new school board term, the *Cincinnati Star-Times* stated,

> *This gladsome new year is leap year, woman's year if you please. So it was that, at the meeting Monday, at 10:30 o'clock, of the new Board of Education, Miss M. Edith Campbell was the target of all eyes. Her advent into that assembly of men, however, was as simple as though she had been a member of such a body for six terms and has as "honorable colleagues" a dozen women. 'The Campbells have come,' said a gallant gentleman. True there was only one of the famous clan present.*[22]

Once on that board, Edith worked hard for four years to upgrade education standards for students and staff. Edith helped conceive of the idea of a vocation bureau.[22] Included in this were counseling programs, vocational guidance and placement, physical and psychological exams, educational measurement and testing, protection and services for the physically and mentally challenged. She developed preventative measures for the first signs of juvenile delinquency and scholarships for the able and deserving. These last she begun during the First World War to encourage boys and girls to resist the temptation to leave school for well-paid war jobs and instead to continue their education to prepare themselves for more responsible and permanent work.

It was all of this incredible dedication to the cause of vocational education that led to her consideration in *The Ladies Home Journal* of 1915 mentioned at the beginning of this chapter. That article stated:

> *All through the Middle West Miss Campbell is recognized as an authority on progressive educational matters. Her efficiency has been so thoroughly demonstrated that last Autumn Governor Cox chose her as a member of the School Survey Commission. Again, she is the first woman to hold such position. That Commission reported its statewide investigations in a special session of the Ohio legislature. Laws have since been enacted which bid fair to revolutionize education in rural schools in Ohio.*[23]

Still, the puzzle of Edith Campbell's life has so many pieces, so many directions of concern for the well being of others, that this chapter can only hint at the wonder of the final picture. In 1930 Edith Campbell chaired the White House Conference on Child Health and Protection. She was a charter member of the American Association of Social Workers. She helped organize the Negro Welfare Association that became the Urban League.

She was also a part of the inception of the Juvenile Protective Association and the Helen S. Trounstine Foundation for Social Research.

Beyond the local horizon was her concern for the peace of the world in the midst of a world war and so she was a voice of the

Cincinnati Peace League. She was also a strong local advocate for the call for a World Court. Note of her participation in both of these causes brought mention in the *New York Times*.[24] When President Woodrow Wilson came to Cincinnati to call for a "society of nations," Edith Campbell was one of his two escorts. Writes Betty Van Meter Ames, "Much as she hated war, she loved a good fight, but never a personal one, always for principles, for minority groups or the underdog. She supported academic freedom and civil liberties no matter how unpopular her stand or what vituperation came her way."[25]

M. Edith Campbell, woman advocate in a man's world

Photo: Library of Congress

In 1931 Edith Campbell was the first woman to receive the University of Cincinnati's Distinguished Alumnae award along with the honorary degree of doctor of humanities. *The Cincinnati Times-Star* of June 13, 1931, quoted Dr. S. Gail Lowrie, Professor of Political Science at Cincinnati University who presented her award and degree, "I have the honor to present one of the most distinguished alumnae of the University of Cincinnati, Miss Edith Campbell. It is given to few people to exert so great an influence in molding the educational and social institutions of a great city…..For her skill in dealing with problems of social adjustment in both State and Nation, she has won deserved recognition, and stands as a conspicuous leader among the women of her generation."[26]

In 1933 Edith was appointed by Governor George White as trustee of Ohio State University. She then became the first woman to chair that committee and perhaps was the first woman to hold such a position in the nation. It was not an easy time to lead a university as the world was heading into war and the United States was enduring the Depression. In it all was the controversy of the Communist Party and the right of free speech on campus.

A group of fifteen students petition the University to have a Communist club on campus. The request came to the Board of Trustees where Edith and Lockwood Thompson stood against the majority decision that refused recognition of such group on campus. Edith not only spoke out at the meeting of her firm conviction for free speech for all but voiced her opinion to the whole university community. Justice Felix Frankfurter of the U.S. Supreme Court wrote to Lockwood Thompson, "I am fond of quoting T. H. Huxley's definition of a university as 'the fortress of the higher life of a nation.' Never has it been more necessary to see that fortress is maintained and strengthened in its spiritual forces. Therefore I rejoice over the stand taken by you and Miss Campbell as manifested in your dissenting report of August 15th. The implications of that document seem to me to be the test of wise direction for a university."[27]

Mindful of such a rich, passionate, and determined advocacy for justice, we revisit the quip made in the *Ladies Home Journal* article that Edith's life was "enough to fill a book." It

*Edith Campbell and Colleagues
of the Ohio State University Board of Trustees*

Photo: Cincinnati Historical Society

is interesting that for the number of times commentators on Edith's life have mentioned that line, that no such book was ever written.

It is hard to imagine that a book could be written on Edith's life alone. Her life was intertwined with her sister who was not just making daily rounds at the hospital while her sister took on the world.

Dr. Elizabeth Campbell was as obsessed with public health issues as her sister was for public education. Elizabeth's work in the woman's prison with prostitutes made her very aware of the impact of sexually transmitted diseases. To have a woman doctor addressing venereal disease in an open, objective and analytical manner was a phenomenon in 1917 as was her organization of the local Social Hygiene Association where she served as its first president. She was instrumental in both closing down the red-light district of Cincinnati and treating those who were transmitting the disease.[28]

But venereal diseases were not the only communicable disease with which Elizabeth was concerned. Tuberculosis was terribly out of hand in Cincinnati. In 1909 it had the second highest rate of tuberculosis in the United States. A large part of the problem was the lack of health care for the poor. The city needed public health nursing and Elizabeth made it happen. The Visiting Nurses Association was established with Elizabeth as its chair and soon it was addressing not only tuberculosis but a terrible scourge of scarlet fever.

When the city of Cincinnati was getting on top of communicable diseases, Elizabeth turned her efforts towards the promotion of planned parenthood. "Children should only come into this world when they are wanted."[29] She stood for birth control at a time when it was not even a matter of allowed public discussion. In 1929 the City of Cincinnati decided to investigate the feasibility of a Women's Health Clinic. One of the four physicians selected to pursue the issue was Elizabeth Campbell. From this effort emerged the Maternal Health Clinic that over the years would emerge as a part of Children's Hospital.[30]

The commitment of Elizabeth Campbell in addressing the issues of communicable diseases did not come without a heavy price. *The Ohio State Medical Journal* noted that during the diphtheria epidemics of her early practice, she relentlessly pursued an unusual case of the disease to prove it the cause of the patient's death. Her dogged determination to get to the bottom of this one case led to her contracting the disease herself, which required a nine-month recuperation and lifelong complications of heart problems.[31]

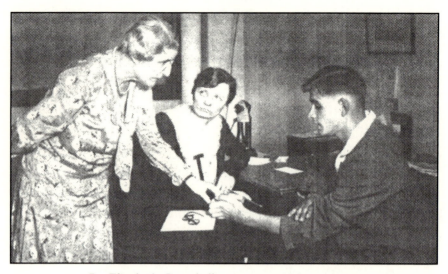

Dr. Elizabeth Campbell, consummate diagnostician

Her gifts as a physician led the American Medical Association to describe her as "one of the best educated and foremost of American women practitioners."³² In her later years Elizabeth became the recipient of many awards. Christ Hospital unveiled a portrait of Elizabeth, their first woman staff member, the first woman physician in Cincinnati. The Academy of Medicine recognized:

> ...her vision, her executive ability, her power to work indefatigably, and to fight, if necessary, for human welfare. But that is only part. She was deeply interested in the welfare of each individual with whom she had association. She gave of herself unsparingly to her patients, to the Christ Hospital nurses whom she counseled, to her friends. She was a brilliant diagnostician. To the sick room she brought strength and reassurance, and often laughter, for she was essentially a gay person. Her zest for life was contagious. The good effects of civic reforms she started continue, tangible witness to her great ability. In the hearts of those who knew her she will be remembered for more

intangible qualities: her vitality and charm, for her loving kindness.[33]

Elizabeth would not die from her heart concerns but from cancer. On June 7, 1945, she wrote a letter that she was beginning "the great adventure of dying."[34] In a few months she would die in her sister's care.

Edith Campbell lived until 1962. Seven years after her death came the dedication of the M. Edith Campbell Junior High School of Cincinnati. At that dedication it was remembered that President Taft called Edith Campbell, "Ohio's leading woman citizen." It further noted the feeling of many that she "was the leading woman citizen of Cincinnati." The dedication concluded, "It seemed appropriate that one of the schools she loved should be named in her honor."[35]

Marguerite W. Zapolean, in her essay on the Campbell sisters in *Queen City Heritage,* made the following conclusion regarding these two Campbell sisters and the link of one's heritage to one's accomplishment:

> *In their veins flowed the blood of ancestors who crusaded, or more often worked quietly, for better government, education, and daily living. They carried on family tradition when they recognized and tackled some of the problems that prompted Lincoln Steffens in 1905 to proclaim Cincinnati 'the worst-governed city in the United States.'*[36]

Such tribute to the crusading spirit of ancestral "blood in the veins" gives us reason to ask "what crusade?" On what ancestral conviction was passion born for such outspoken and visionary reform? The answer to such questions is a culminating chapter of this book. Before we examine the question and its answer, we need to consider the life of the final son of William and Elizabeth Campbell who was actually their first born.

Dr. Elizabeth Campbell

Cincinnati Historical Society

*Portrait of Edith by Carolyn Von Stein
painted for the dedication of
M. Edith Campbell Junior High School*

Cincinnati Historical Society

CHAPTER 9
JAMES W. CAMPBELL

William Campbell   Elizabeth Wilson Campbell
James, *Charles, John W., Joseph N., Elizabeth, Mary, Rebecca, Samuel, Phoebe, Sarah, Fidelia*

James W. Campbell, the oldest son of William and Elizabeth, is saved for the last because it is through James and wife Mary that the flow of the story finds its final chapters.

When William and Elizabeth decided to leave and start again in Ohio in 1799, all eleven children followed, except James. James stayed behind as a bachelor, then husband and father. He farmed northeast of the family home in Fleming county on Johnson's Fork of the Licking River, fifteen miles south of Maysville. When William and Elizabeth moved to Ohio they were thirty miles away from James. Then again, if the move to Ohio did not turn out, there was always the oldest son to fall back on only thirty miles away. James would remain in Kentucky for twenty-six years after the rest of the family moved on.

Kentucky was not for James what it was to the rest of the family. Remembering the witness of third son John W. Campbell, Kentucky meant dirt poor. Austerity followed William and Elizabeth, at least until the last years of their lives. Son James, however, seems to have made a go of it. He stuck with Kentucky until it proved out.

When William Campbell died in 1822, he left in his will one hundred dollars for each of his eleven children, except for sons Congressman John W. Campbell and eldest son James W.

Campbell. Both of them received five dollars. The most likely explanation was that both of these sons were self-sustaining as to not need such inheritance. When James W. Campbell finally did move to Brown County, Ohio, three years after his father's death, he was able to purchase the farm of Samuel McConaughy near Georgetown, Ohio, which was one of the more desirable farmlands in the region. He soon added to that initial investment to what became a farm of nearly 900 acres. This would have been a sizable farm from its day well into the twentieth century. In the biography of James' son John Milton Campbell, mention is made of John's fondness for agriculture. Had John M. stayed with the farming operation instead of becoming a missionary, the book suggests John certainly would have made do, if not become a wealthy farmer.[1] Whereas William could not afford school books for his son, James W. put his son John through Miami University (Ohio) and then Lane Theological Seminary.

All of this suggests a picture of changing family fortune, perhaps reflecting the overall progress of the region from frontier to established society. It also gives us our first index into the life of this eldest son.

Bachelor life in Kentucky lasted two years for James after the family left for Ohio. On January 7, 1801, at the age of twenty-six, James married Mary "Polly" Duncan. David Duncan, her father was the bondsman.[2] Mary was the twelfth of fourteen children of David Duncan Sr. Then again, what did that mean? A marriage is the merging of two rivers into one, so who were the Duncans that flowed new life into the Campbell Saga?

Twenty years ago the question was answered by a genealogist from Mason County, Kentucky. She copied the will of David Duncan and a genealogy of his descendants. A grandson of David wrote the following summary of his grandfather David Duncan. It reads as follows:

David Duncan was by birth and education a

Scotchman and took active part in the Rebellion of 1745. He was at the battle of Preston-Pass and during the year succeeding was in the sanguinary action at Culloden and surviving the terrible defeat which his party sustained in this action he still followed the uncertain fortunes of Prince Charles throughout the year 1746 until his leader left Scotland destitute of means and friends. He made his way to the Colonies of America, having been included in the royal proclamation offering a reward for his apprehension for Charles and his adherents if taken in Scotland. He first settled in Massachusetts and again felt the sting of British lead at Bunker Hill. He subsequently served in the American Army throughout the Revolution. Peace restored, he settled with his wife in Carlisle, Pennsylvania, where he raised a large family, some of whom rose to honorable distinction. Some years later he removed with the younger portion of his family to Mason County, Kentucky, and was engaged with Simon Kenton in the bloody and thrilling incidents which distinguished the history of the early settlement of that state.[3]

I remember at the time thinking that Grandfather David Duncan must have been a character. He certainly seemed larger than life—in fact too much so. To cram such heroic living into one lifetime suggested the merging of two generations of father and son. There was, after all, a David Duncan Jr. (Ennis Duncan). Mention of this family tale of Grandfather Duncan was included in earlier drafts of this text as an example of the exaggeration we bring to merged generations until one person becomes the ancestral Paul Bunyan.

The former draft and its casual reference to Mary's Duncan ancestors was submitted for proofreading to historian Virginia Bryant of Ironton, Ohio, whose quick response was a question.

"Your Mary Duncan is related to David Duncan, *the* David Duncan the frontiersman?"

My knowledge of early American frontiersmen extends little beyond the popularized lives of Daniel Boone and Simon Kenton. I had hoped to make connection between Simon Kenton and William Campbell as they both were dwelling in the Blue Licks region of Kentucky at the same time. No direct connection was found. What was found, was a book called *The Frontiersmen* by Allan W. Eckert. My cousin Allan Campbell had been reading it and thought I might find something in it for this research. It was, in fact, the very book that Virginia Bryant was now suggesting I read to understand who David Duncan, *the* David Duncan was.

The book includes this encounter with Simon Kenton, sixteen years old, in the company of Jacob Greathouse and others. They were sitting in a tavern when a stranger walked in...

July 29, 1771 - Monday Night

The stranger strode across the room as he spoke and now stopped where the lamplight struck him fully. He was a striking figure of a man. Of medium height and well proportioned, he carried himself with a boundless assurance. Thick glossy black hair crept from beneath the raccoon skin cap he wore and curled to his shoulders. His buckskins were well worn, yet as clean as any Simon had seen worn on this frontier. His features were not at all rough as Simon had come to expect of border men. If anything, they tended to be close to the line, where they cease being strikingly handsome and become "pretty." The saving grace in this unusual fact was a pair of the most intense eyes Simon had ever seen. They moved incessantly, noting every characteristic of their surroundings until, that taken care of, they locked on any object unfamiliar with a scrutiny so penetrating that it seemed no amount of camouflage could hide the truth from his gaze...Simon realized he was witnessing something rare indeed - Jacob Greathouse exhibiting unabashed friendship for a fellow human being. 'Dave!' he roared. 'Dave Duncan! By God, where you been...'... Had Simon been impressed with the newcomer's bearing and appearance, he was infinitely more so at the man's name. David Duncan! It would be a great warrior who could lift this man's raven scalp. In the borderlands where many men seemed giants among average people, this man was a giant among giants... Few frontiersmen indeed made names for themselves which were recognizable outside the border area's and those who did could almost be counted on one hand. Simon had heard of only three before leaving Fauquier County. One, of course was his Uncle Tom, who really didn't count; the other two, however, had a fame which preceded them greatly. One was John Finley, whose activities in Southwestern Virginia were already legendary. The other was the famous scout and trader of Western Pennsylvania and the Middle Ground who now extended his hand in welcome.

Simon took the firm grip offered and responded in kind, unabashed admiration reflected in his voice. 'Mr. Duncan! I've heard an awful lot about you, sir. It is an honor to meet you.'[4]

    I read the excerpts in stunned silence, first to the wonder of Simon Kenton in awe of David Duncan, who it seems amidst his contemporaries was indeed larger than life. Second was the wonder of the rich stories that must have filled the house of Mary and James W. Campbell whose farm bordered the lands of David Duncan in his old age.

James and Mary Duncan Campbell had seven children, three sons and four daughters. Nancy Campbell, Elizabeth Campbell, Washington G. Campbell, Eliza Campbell, Hiram Campbell, John Milton Campbell, and Jane D. Campbell. When James and Mary moved to Brown County, Ohio, in 1825, their children, now grown, joined the migration and lived near their parents' new home as did Mary's sister Jane Duncan. Later, when Jane Duncan decided to sell her portion of her father's estate, she gave her nephew Washington G. Campbell the power of attorney.[5] Letters speak fondly of visits of Mary's children to her brother Martin Duncan.[6]

James and Mary Campbell's Brown County home located two miles east of Georgetown on the Hillman Ridge Road

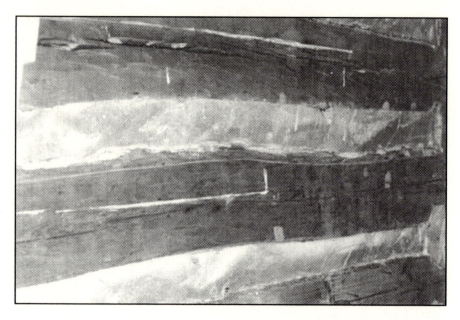

The heavy oak logs of the house revealed in the interior walls

The Pennsylvania Dutch barn built in 1819 with a fifty-foot central beam of walnut.

James W. Campbell

School land was given by the Campbells for the rural school, which is now a private residence

Besides farming, James also constructed "wind mills." These were not devices to pump water. Rather, they sifted wheat. They also cause us to remember a reference made about James' uncle Joseph N. Campbell who ran for the state legislature and was deemed one "who was set to making windmills and watching wolves." Perhaps these windmills were an inherited family trade. We find reference to the sale of these "wheat fans" in the Georgetown newspaper at the cost of sixteen to eighteen dollars. Note as well the reference directly below the wheat fans for a "pressing call" for creditors to pay up at Jesse Grant's store in Georgetown. Jesse Grant was the father of Ulysses S. Grant.

Though we do not have a likeness of the windmills made by James W. Campbell, there are similar examples.

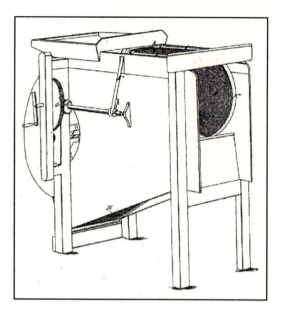

A wheat fan

Wheat Fans

OF a superior quality, made of good materials, and kept for sale, at the residence of the subscriber, two miles east of Georgetown. Price, from $16 to $18.

JAMES W. CAMPBELL.

May 8, 1833.   47

Pressing Call.

BEING much pressed for money, I would most earnestly request all those indebted to me, to make immediate payment.

J. R. GRANT.

Georgetown, May 7, 1833.   47-p

Campbell Wheat Fans for sale[7]
Note in lower ad the call to creditors by Jesse Grant,
father of Ulysses S. Grant.

Besides wheat fans, James W. Campbell also solicited surrounding farmers for the service of his bulls.

Durham Bulls for lease[8]
The advertisement mistakenly typed J.M. instead of J.W. Campbell

Home Forgotten

✱ ✱ ✱ ✱ ✱ ✱ ✱ ✱ ✱

The winds of religious revival were blowing again in the early 1800s in what was known as "The Second Great Awakening." Caught up in that spirit of renewal were James and Mary.

James and Mary Duncan Campbell were devoted to their faith. James was a trustee of the Straight Creek Presbyterian Church that became the Georgetown Presbyterian Church.[9] Their devotion was revealed in the introduction to the biography of their son, John Milton Campbell:

> *He [John], enjoyed the best advantages for his early education which the schools of the neighborhood afforded, nor did his parents consider that in furnishing him these, their whole duty was discharged. They were careful also to educate him at home by superintending and aiding in his mental culture, and more especially by training him in the knowledge of religious truth and in the practice of religious duties. Here we may find the origin of his usefulness and his excellence. Whatever beneficial influences may have been exerted upon him elsewhere, it was under the paternal roof, and in the family circle, as he used gratefully to acknowledge, that those seeds of divine truth were sown in his heart which afterwards yielded, through God's grace, such a harvest of peace and joy to his soul, and which we may add, yielded such abundant fruit to the good of man, and to the glory of God."*[10]

The piety of the "Second Great Awakening" led Presbyterians deeper into a life of austere and solemn devotion expressed now in abstention of alcohol. For some in the Campbell family, this went too far. Brother Judge John W. Campbell, himself a formidable proponent of the moral and industrious life in the Calvinist spirit, looked with a jaundiced eye on his older brother James' religiosity. John makes the following acerbic comment to his wife's nephew in attending a wedding of James and Mary's daughter Eliza.

November 11, 1827.

….. James Ralston and Eliza Campbell my brother James W.'s daughter were married on Thursday (and) was a wash. We were all there except Mitchell. There were nearly 100 persons present. We had a good dinner, but Presbyterian abstinence interdicted the use of ardent spirits, hence the company was grave and sober: and without any striking demonstrations of mirth…….. It must have been a ghastly wedding when so many long faces were present.[11]

James W.'s son, John Milton Campbell, gives further definition to the meaning of grave and sober when he told of the impact of worship at the Georgetown church. "….the faithful preaching of Mr. K. began to arouse my early impressions. The word spoken was often an arrow to my heart….as communion seasons would return and the Savior's dying love again be celebrated, I felt myself to be an excuseless murderer, numbered among the murderers of the only Savior, and justly lying under their condemnation."[12]

In such a spirit of conviction, son John found his calling and enrolled at Miami University of Ohio in Oxford, Ohio, to prepare himself for the ministry. His ardent desire to preach the gospel could not wait until graduation from seminary. John began to preach what he heard—beginning with or on his family. He cast a critical eye on each one of his siblings, determining whether this brother or sister was indeed saved by the faith and let them know of his concern. In a long letter to his brother Hiram, John solicited Hiram's conscience to determine if Hiram had indeed been convicted of his sins and was certain of his salvation. Was he sure he was not on his way to hell?[13]

Brother Hiram did not answer for some time. When he did respond it was to let his little brother know, thank you very much, but that he did not care for the hellfire and damnation of grave and sober preachers and he did not care for his brother's interrogation of his spiritual life.[14]

Brother John Milton replied in a letter of March 4, 1837, "If you are indeed a Christian and endeavoring to live in his holy life I can not see why you have such an aversion to appeals directed to the conscience, whether given in private or from the pulpit."[15] This exchange between brothers speaks of the spiritual concerns in the James Campbell home. They also give context to the chapter that follows as spiritual values become expressed as social concern.

* * * * * * * * *

When John Campbell of Ironton was trying to persuade Mary's son Hiram to come and join him in the formation of Ironton, he mentioned that Hiram should bring his mother along to survey the situation. John also mentioned that Mary would be well suited to move to Ironton.[16]

If Mary ever made the trip to Ironton before 1855, she would have found her son Hiram well suited to care for her. Her every need would have been met. It would have been for her the good life. Mary did not, however, move to Ironton. She chose instead to move west to yet another frontier, starting all over on the plains of Illinois. She was then in her seventies.

One hundred years later Mary's great-grandchildren were trying to identify the first photographs of the family. One intriguing photograph identified as Eleanor Jane Lilley Campbell, daughter-in-law of Mary just could not be Eleanor Jane Campbell. It is an extremely early photograph that was sketched over to draw out the highlights of a picture that had little contrast. The picture has been taken to photo archivists and compared to the one known photo of Eleanor Jane Lilley. It definitely was not Eleanor Jane. Then who could it be? What Campbell would be of that advanced age at these early years of photography? Again and again we come back to the likelihood that the photo is of Mary Campbell, wife of James W. Campbell. We include this photo with a question mark, in hopes that future research might further identify the picture conclusively.

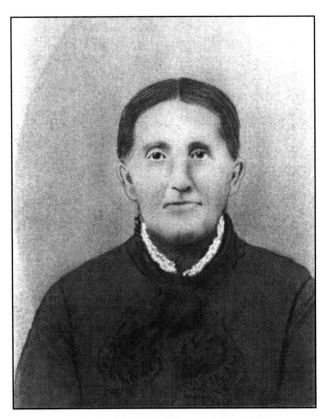

Mary Duncan Campbell ?

James died in 1850 at the age of seventy-five. In his estate settlement we find reference to his final medical bill of sixteen dollars. How much simpler life and death were in the mid-nineteenth century. That same estate settlement mentioned three hundred fifty dollars given to wife Mary Campbell for her "maintenance," almost a dollar a day.

James W. Campbell was buried at the cemetery at the west end of Georgetown. When the gravestone was rediscovered in the early 1980s, it was leaning at more than a forty-five degree angle. When Dr. Allan Campbell found it again in 1999, it had completely fallen over. Allan had the stone restored with a marker beside to designate the grave since the words of the original were fast becoming illegible.

James David Campbell at the grave of his distant namesake James W. Campbell, Old Georgetown Cemetery.

Mary Duncan Campbell lived until 1863. Her home with son Washington G. Campbell is now most of Mt. Hope Cemetery, extending into what became the newly emerging town of Champaign, Illinois, and encompassing what would be the southern edge of the campus of the University of Illinois.

＊＊＊＊＊＊＊＊＊

THE CHILDREN OF JAMES W. AND MARY CAMPBELL

THE FOUR SISTERS

James W. and Mary Campbell had four daughters and three sons. Of the four daughters we know when they were born, who they married, their children, and when they died. All four sisters were lost to the oral tradition of the family. The first efforts of reconstructing a family lineage in 1960 did not mention them. That is—except for one thing.

The first daughter, Nancy, was born in 1802. At the age of twenty-six Nancy married James McIlhenny in a service performed by Rev. John Rankin. The McIlhennys lived two farms away from James and Mary and in 1830 provided the first grandchild in the family, a daughter named for her grandmother Mary. Two other children were born to Nancy before her husband died in the 1840s. When her father, James W., died in 1850, Nancy moved to the home place to care for her mother.

The second daughter, Elizabeth Campbell, named for her grandmother Elizabeth was born in 1804 and married Duncan Evans. They had two children, George and Eliza, and lived a mile down the road from James and Mary. Their daughter Eliza died in 1855 at the age of twenty. Elizabeth's husband Duncan died three years after their daughter's death. With her husband's death, Elizabeth Campbell Evans moved to Champaign, Illinois, to be with her mother Mary and brother Washington.

Eliza, the third daughter was born December 14, 1807. She

too was married in a service performed by Rev. John Rankin on November 1, 1827. This was the "dour wedding" of Eliza and James Ralston previously mentioned by John W. Campbell. Eliza and James had three children. Joseph Milton, Mary J., and Wilson J. Ralston. Mary J. died in childhood. Eliza Campbell Ralston lived to the age of eighty-five dying in Brown County December 20, 1892. She and her husband were buried in the same cemetery as Eliza's father, James W. Campbell.

The fourth daughter was Jane Campbell born in 1814. Jane married William P. Marklem. They had one child, Jane D., who was born the same year her mother died leaving us to wonder if mother Jane might have died in childbirth. Daughter Jane D. herself had a short life, dying at the age of twenty in 1855.

The death of Jane D. exposes an interesting set of coincidences. Elizabeth Campbell Evans and sister Jane Campbell Maklem both bore daughters in 1835. These two cousins named Eliza and Jane D. lived to be twenty years old, dying in the same year of 1855.[17]

Such coincidence of the untimely death of the two cousins of the same age in the same year might give reason for the "one thing" handed on through family tradition regarding the daughters of James and Mary. That is not so. No, what is remembered is the family of the sister Eliza.

To understand all of this, we must jump ahead one hundred thirty years and four generations. We must go to the very beginning of the research of this book and the gathering of information from distant and now aging cousins who were handing on what they knew. The year was 1978 and I was talking with my father's cousin Robert Crouch. Bob told the story of Ross Campbell in the Civil War. It was an intriguing story of Ross being captured and dying in Andersonville Prison.

I took cousin Bob's story at face value. The problem is that face value didn't prove out. There was no record of any

Ross Campbell serving from Brown County, Ohio. There was no record of any Ross Campbell dying at Andersonville Prison. With great reluctance, I shared with cousin Bob that the family story just didn't pan out. No mention is made of Ross Campbell in any census or military record. Bob was all the more adamant that it was so. He remembered his mother telling it over and over again. To this day I have kept the file of Ross Campbell as a memory of cousin Bob and a lesson in family history.

It was many years later, after cousin Bob had died, that the puzzle parts came together. On the surface, the handed-down family story was off the mark. Indeed, there was no Ross Campbell in the family. There were, however, the two sons, the only living children of Eliza Campbell Ralston. In 1862 both brothers became a part of Company C of the 89th Ohio Infantry—the ill-fated 89th Ohio Infantry.

Commanded by an incompetent colonel and on maneuvers for thirteen months without real combat experience, three hundred fifty men of the 89th Infantry were suddenly plunged into the battle of Chickamauga to try and prop up an already disastrous, bloody loss by the Union Army. The 89th Infantry did not receive the order to withdraw. Trapped, many of those who survived, including both sons of Eliza Campbell Ralston, were marched off to prisoner of war camps. Fifty-six men of the Ohio 89th Infantry died at Andersonville including both sons of Eliza Campbell Ralston. They died of starvation and dysentry a month apart. Wilson died June 15th and Joseph died July 16th, 1864.[18] The mention of Sergeant W. Ralston's death in the *Ripley Bee* Newspaper in December of 1864 simply mentions his name along with two others of the area who died in that prison.

There was no Ross Campbell who died at Andersonville. No, it was worse than that. It was both sons, all the family "Aunt Ralston" had left. That the story would be passed on for four generations speaks of its impact. That Ralston became Ross speaks once more of the blur that comes with family stories handed on generation to generation. I only wish cousin Bob had lived long enough to know the real story.

HIRAM CAMPBELL

Hiram Campbell, the second son and fourth child of James and Mary Campbell was born in Fleming County, Kentucky, in November, 1810. He moved with the family to Brown County, Ohio, in 1825 and five years later at the age of twenty published the Hillsboro *Gazette*. While living in Hillsboro, Hiram met and married Rachel Starr. Rachel was a niece of David Trimble of Trimble Iron Works in Greenup County, Kentucky, and it was at the Argillite Furnace of this company that Hiram began work as a bookkeeper.

Hiram's wife Rachel only lived a short time after their marriage. With her death Hiram's allegiance began to wane towards Rachel's uncle and the iron industry. He was not happy in Kentucky. Correspondence from his younger brother John Milton Campbell suggested that Hiram might give thought to going back into the publishing business. John M. also suggested that he knew some eligible women in the Walnut Hills area of Cincinnati that might make for a good prospect of a new relationship.[19]

In fact, however, it was not his brother but his cousin John C. Campbell of the Mount Vernon Furnace in Lawrence County, Ohio, who opened the door to Hiram's future. Hiram left Kentucky for Ohio and began to work for his cousin as a bookkeeper, eventually becoming the manager of the Mount Vernon Furnace. The relationship between the cousins has already been addressed in a previous chapter. John was boss, at least in the beginning. In time Hiram not only became an ironmaster on his terms but explored his own avenues of interest as well.

While cousin John was refining the iron-making process and building new iron furnaces, Hiram threw his hat into the ring of politics. Hiram was a representative to the 1842-1843 sessions of the Ohio legislature. One term of this was enough. Being a legislator was not his cup of tea. Hiram was noted for saying regarding the legislature meeting every year, "We don't want any legislature. The people are opposed to it. Once in two years is enough." His strong Republican leanings continued through his years in Ironton until his business days were over.

It is a moment often repeated in Ironton History that Rutherford B. Hayes stayed at the home of Hiram Campbell during Hayes' campaign for the presidency of the United States. A closer look reveals that if that is true, it certainly wasn't the first time. Hayes also stayed at the Hiram Campbell home during an earlier campaign for Ohio Governor. In a letter written in Hiram Campbell's home Hayes writes to his wife:

> *Sunday A.M. August 1st, 1875.*
>
> *I came into town (Ironton) covered with mud and tead with Mrs. Enochs. Am now at the finest home, Hiram Campbell's where I stopped in 1867... 1P.M. at the Presbyterian Church with Mrs. Campbell and daughter...* [20]

In 1849 Hiram affirmed his cousin's request and became a stock-holder in the Ohio Iron and Coal Company and with that became one of the founders of Ironton. Hiram was also one of the organizers of the Iron Railroad. He invested in the building of a foundry and was one of the organizers of the Big Sandy Packet Company that shipped freight up and down the Ohio River between Cincinnati and Pomeroy. To be sure, the spirit and momentum of the time lay with his cousin John whose energy and vision seemed to have no limits. John set the agenda. Yet, within the overall vision of John, Hiram found his own way until, with his sons and sons-in-law he founded the firm of H. Campbell and Sons. They maintained the Mount Vernon Furnace and built Sarah Furnace in Ironton (most likely named for Hiram's second wife). It was the most up-to-date furnace operation of its day. Hiram was also involved in the operation of the Howard Furnace.

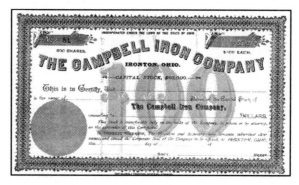

*A stock certificate for the "Campbell Iron Company"
run by Hiram Campbell and his children*

Courtesy Lawrence County Historical Society

*Hiram Campbell
April 4, 1863*

Eventually Hiram retired from business and turned his interest to the solitude of raising a garden. Hiram came to live for the joy of flowers and the delight in the color and fragrance of the cuttings he brought into his home from his efforts with the earth.

In 1892 Hiram's wife Sarah died. Hiram's world became more withdrawn in a very large and now quiet home. It was in this loss that Hiram found solace in the company of old friends Lovead T. Dean and Cyrus Ellison. These elders of the town shared daily adventures to ponder the world of industry they had played such a roll to secure. Fortunately, L.T. Dean kept a diary of these daily outings as the men made jaunts around Ironton to inspect, deliberate, and offer their critique of the furnaces and mills of the area.[21]

Once, Hiram, L.T., and Cyrus delighted in the free passage they received on the Iron Railroad and the kindness of attention afforded them to inspect the operation of the Lawrence Furnace. On another outing the trio strolled passed the Eagle Mill and over to the Belfort Furnace, determining the operation was just not progressing at a pace equal to ability. Still, on another day's excursion of the mills so much excitement happened that L. T. didn't have time to record it.

Not all of these outings were focused on industry. Some days were given to taking in a case on trial at the County Court House and one day was given to their own pursuit of justice as they brought to the attention of the probate judge the no-good antics of one Billy Barlow.

L.T. Dean writes of an evening outing after dinner to take in a passing entertainment. "Mr. Hiram Campbell and myself went to the circus grounds and saw one of the side shows, consisting of one fat woman and some other curiosities and had quite a good time." On another occasion the good spirit of the day was found in the surprise birthday party for L.T. Dean. The gathered guests, including Hiram Campbell, spent a part of the evening conducting a business meeting on L.T.'s birthday. They determined that the combined age of the L.T.'s gathered friends was five hundred fifty-five years and thus making the average age of those celebrating at seventy-two.

There were also quiet days, as the weather demanded, and these elders of the town would venture only as far as the general store for conversation and then retreat to the comfort of their individual hearths. In it all L. T. Dean made more than one reference to his appreciation of Hiram Campbell. Once he framed that appreciation in a comparison. "Mr. Hiram Campbell and myself took quite a long walk down to the bridge over the mouth of the creek and I must say that he is a far more interesting partner than Cyrus Ellison, for Mr. Campbell has a larger fund to draw from than Cyrus has and he is uniformly better posted on all subjects that we generally conversed upon."

Not all of the outings of these men went without public note. On May 6, 1894, *The Ironton Republican* gave this account of an excusion upriver:

> *Yesterday, Mr. Hiram Campbell and Mr. L.T. Dean took a trip up river aboard the Georgia, as far as Ashland, and also took a ride over the electric car line of that city and expressed themselves as delighted with its equipment and operation. They returned by way of the ferry and street car line from Coal Grove to Ironton, regarding which service they have few words of commendation. These gentlemen never travel with their eyes shut but are close and accurate observers of things around them. To the 'Republican' they said that it seemed strange to them that Ironton, with five times as much travel and business along its car line as has the Ashland line, should be compelled to put up with such inferior car service. They also came home*

thoroughly imbued with the idea that as a business point, Ironton can not be excelled.

Six months after this trip to Ashland, L.T. Dean died. Hiram Campbell was an honorary pallbearer. Hiram himself would live two more years with his death coming in August, 1896. He was still walking the streets of Ironton until the day before he died.

Left to mourn Hiram were his children. His son John W. Campbell carried on the family management of the Mount Vernon Furnace. John was also a soldier in the Civil War. Joseph H. Campbell was a popular newspaper columnist of the Cincinnati *Commercial Tribune*. Son Harry H. Campbell ran the Ironton Wood Mantel Company. Daughter Maria married John Moulton who was key to running the Sarah Furnace when it was in the family business. Finally, there was daughter Minnie who married B. M. Caldwell.

On the occasion of Hiram's death *The Ironton Weekly* stated:

Mr. Campbell was a man of gentle nature, who all his life enjoyed the friendship and confidence of all who knew him. He was charitable in the broadest and fullest sense of the word, and hundreds of needy ones have been benefited and had their burdens lightened by his kindly aid, so quietly and unostentatiously bestowed, that few but the recipients knew of it.[22]

* * * * * * * * *

JOHN MILTON CAMPBELL

Hiram Campbell left behind two memorable architectural tributes to the city of Ironton. One was his home of over twenty rooms, a French Second Empire manor with a distinctive mansord roof.

*Hiram Campbell's home in Ironton.
Hiram's home together with cousin John Campbell's home
formed a single city block.*

The second was Hiram's gift to Ironton's First Presbyterian Church. Four round stained-glass windows in the east wall of the sanctuary pivot a central small window. The windows receive each day the burst of morning light that radiates a warm glow through the Geneva vaulted sanctuary. Together the windows suggest an open rose, a flower in full bloom, a flower of remembrance by Hiram to his brother John Milton Campbell, missionary to Africa.

James W. Campbell

The Rose Windows of the First Presbyterian Church of Ironton given by Hiram Campbell in honor of his brother, The Rev. John Milton Campbell

The year 1835 was memorable for the two brothers. Hiram moved to the Hanging Rock region of Ohio to begin to make his mark in the iron industry. That same year, his twenty-three-year-old brother John, left the family farm in Brown County and the material trappings of this world to prepare not only for ministry but the rigors of being a missionary to the far corners of the world. To that end, John was even more consumed to his cause than his brother and cousin were to iron. John Milton Campbell did not just go into the ministry, he gave himself to ministry with such an intense, passionate, singular vision that little else mattered. Upon John's death *The Missionary Herald* noted:

> *Mr. Campbell was eminently fitted for the missionary work. His piety was of the most active and self-denying kind. He sought not his own but the good of others. His remarkable simplicity of character, amiable*

manners, and affectionate disposition, soon secured the confidence and won the esteem with all whom he came in contact. But the most prominent trait in his character was his single devotion to the cause of missions.[23]

John Campbell's biographer would later state, "...the zeal with which he exhibited in the cause of Christ, and the singleness of purpose with which he devoted himself to its advancement, were extraordinary."[24]

THE
TRUE MISSIONARY SPIRIT,
AS EXEMPLIFIED IN
THE LIFE AND TRIUMPHANT DEATH
OF
JOHN MILTON CAMPBELL,
LATE MISSIONARY TO AFRICA.
BY R. W. WILSON.

Cincinnati:
GEORGE L. WEED,
AT THE BIBLE, TRACT, AND SUNDAY SCHOOL
BOOK DEPOSITORY, NO. 28, WEST 4TH ST.
1847.

The biography of
John Milton Campbell

John M. Campbell quite literally drew the missionary map of the world. John drew a map indicating the presence of the church in each locale around the world and used it for his own lecturing purposes. The Colton Map Company was given a copy of the John Campbell map as John left this country for Africa. The map was mass produced and *The Missionary Herald* of May, 1846 noted, "Mr. Colton has now given permanency to the conception of Mr. Campbell; and wherever these maps are exhibited, they will awaken thoughts of one, who, 'being dead, yet speaketh.' "[25]

R. W. Wilson's book *The True Missionary Spirit, As exemplified in The Life and Triumphant Death of John Milton Campbell*, was published in 1847. It is from this book that we find focus in John M. Campbell's life. It is a book that begins by noting the family from which John, Hiram, and the other Campbell Children evolved:

> *John Milton Campbell was born in Fleming County, Kentucky, on the 15th of October, 1812 the youngest son of James W. and Mary Campbell. John remained in the state until he was about twelve years of age, when the family removed to the vicinity of Georgetown, Brown County, Ohio, where they are presently residing.*[26]

As noted, John's home was his grounding. In a letter to his parents in March 1840 as he was about to graduate from Miami University of Ohio, he asserts:

> *Your instructions at an early period made a deep impression on my mind, and afterwards seem to have been the great means by which other efforts were in any measure made effectual on my heart. The simple forms of prayer which you taught me were only left off to give place to efforts of my own.*[27]

While living at home John taught a youth Sunday School class. So focused was his concern for these boys in his care that he wrote their names on a piece of paper, "which he would spread out before him as he knelt and prayed for them, one by one, that they might be brought to labor in the Lord's vineyard. Whatever may have been the succeeding history of those boys, they certainly were the subjects of much fervent prayer." It can also be said that wherever John went, even to the ends of the earth, he was always praying for the people back home.

John Milton Campbell was serious and intense. In his intensity John was also deeply impressionable. John's seriousness made him vulnerable. When those he admired fell from grace, they took him with them. When the church proved too human he became disillusioned. Once such disillusionment crushed him to the point he threw out the whole of his faith. "Nay, I even began to doubt the truth of religion, and that there was a God or hereafter....my spirit was troubled, and if I sought God it was with a proud and wayward heart."[28]

It was during this time John said that "I began to long for that peace of mind I once had enjoyed." In the depths of his despair he read an article in the *Philadelphian* (March, 1835) where the King of Bornou in Central Africa was pleading for someone to come and instruct his people in the gospel. John felt a deep peace that such a calling was directed at him. The despair lifted from him and in its place came an extraordinary sense of purpose and conviction. His faith returned with a power of a storm. It also was a faith that marked its progress from the central compass point of his life....home. "It was to prepare for this that I left your family circle and all the worldly comforts and prospects with which you and a kind Providence were surrounding my lot." In John's call to Africa he pleaded for a blessing from those mattered most... "To such a work, dear parents, can you freely give up your son?"[29]

Five years after first reading of the pleading of the King of Bornou, John Milton writes a cousin giving the navigational coordinates of the precise location of Bornou. John is obsessed with this one spot of Africa. "Happy I would be to be instrumental in bringing as rich a blessing to the Sheik of Bornou as God has made him instrumental in bringing (a blessing) to my soul.... His studies are augmented with evangelism constantly talking of Africa and its needs."[30]

As noted, John hones his skills in proclaiming the gospel to less religiously ardent relatives and friends. Daily encounters give reason to witness to the love of God in passing conversation with fellow students. John is not the least bit shy in making the most of a captured audience on a steamboat. He would roll out his big map and begin to lecture to whomever would hear of the great need for missionary outreach to Africa. The publishers of John's biography make a footnote to the text affirming that you could always tell where John M. Campbell had been by the wave of excitement and discussion he left behind.[31]

In 1840 John helps in establishing the first school on the Miami Indian Reserve. That same time he is speaking of the need for missions around his college town of Oxford, Ohio, and addressing the students of South Hanover College, Indiana.

John prepares for the depravation of missions by living in forced austerity. "He appeared to grudge every expense beyond what was strictly necessary." Every extra penny is given to the cause of mission. Additional expense was weighed according to its benefit to Africa. In his seminary studies at Lane Theological Seminary, John justifies an added course in medicine because that will be essential to mission work in Africa. When an aunt offered John twenty-five dollars for a new coat, John would accept it only if in finding a cheaper coat he could give the rest of the money to missions.

While in seminary John was stricken and almost died from some form of hemorrhage. His friends and family saw in this a reason to dissuade him from his passion of missions. The episode left him weaker, more vulnerable to illness. Still, John pressed on finding God's providence in the comment of a doctor that a warmer climate might do him good. He writes a very candid letter to his father saying that he would take his physical well being seriously. "Yet I have felt it my duty to go to a country in which I can not expect to enjoy health, and at most but a few years of life."[32]

Lane Theological Seminary of Cincinnati where John Milton Campbell spent three years preparing to serve as missionary to Africa.

John graduated from Lane Theological Seminary in the spring of 1843. His senior thesis was, "God Accomplishing The Conversion of the World."[33] John was a part of the largest graduating class of the seminary and the commencement exercises bore more people than the chapel could hold.[34]

He spent the next several months lecturing on missions and preparing himself as a missionary for the American Board of Commissioners for Foreign Missions. This board, a cooperative effort between the Congregational and Presbyterian Churches, had decided that John would join his fellow classmate, Albert Bushnell, in serving the new Gaboon Mission Station in the French colony on the coast of west central Africa.

Three days before his ordination, John traveled to Cincinnati for one last reunion with his friends and faculty.

At this gathering at the Second Presbyterian Church, "Mr. Campbell arose, and remarked, that their principle object in appearing, was to say, *farewell.* We have been here three years in the midst of you, prosecuting our profession studies, and receiving instruction. Our hearts have often mingled with yours in devotion to God, and in concerns most intimately connected with his kingdom. Now the time has come for us to leave you, without hope of seeing your faces any more in this world. After a few days, I am to sail for New York to Gaboon in Africa, a station recently taken by Messrs Wilson, Griswold, and Walker, with the most hopeful prospects of doing much in the name of the Lord in that dark land.

"Of all the parts of the world, I choose that as my field of Labor. For eight years I have had my eyes upon it. Now the time has come, and I am in haste to be on my way."[35]

Though John had the credentials of a license to preach for two years, he was not ordained until November 8, 1843, in the Ripley Presbytery of Ohio at which time he was "solemnly set apart to the work of preaching the gospel to the heathen." The day after his ordination John left the family home for Africa. His excitement could scarcely be contained.

One month later in New York, John had finished work for publication of his missionary map and was ready for passage on the ship "Palestine" that would carry Albert Bushnell and himself to Monrovia. "As the time for my departure draws near, my mind is calm—peace, like a river, seems constantly to flow from my bosom." Then he shared words that would echo through the family, even to the reaches of Alaska and the Russian Far East one hundred fifty years later, " I very much desired that each member of our family should possess *a missionary spirit*—a spirit willing to make *any* sacrifice for the cause of Christ."[36]

John stayed in New York and Boston until New Years Day 1844. Albert Bushnell, fellow missionary to Africa stated, "He cheerfully separated from his aged parents and a large circle of friends; and I have never seen him more joyful than when we embarked on board the Palestine, and were rapidly leaving our native shores."[37]

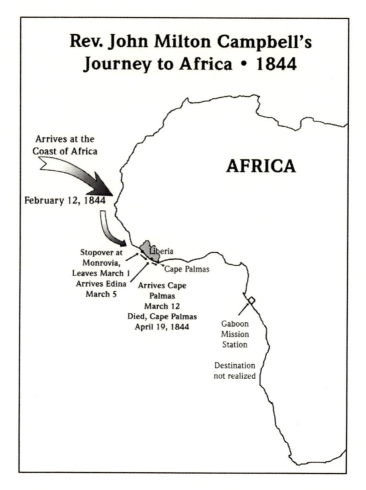

In a few hours his native land was out of sight. With the first attack of sea sickness behind him, John used the voyage to study in depth the climate and geography of Africa. His devotion led him to a disciplined life of prayer seven times a day and as the voyage pressed on, John's intention and spirit grew all the stronger. John wrote, "Since I have been tossing upon the ocean, I have thought of a great many fields of usefulness, which I might have occupied in my native country, but for none of these I would turn back."[38] It is interesting that the stained-glass window in the Ironton Presbyterian Church, depicts the ship with flags blowing in both directions—the love for what he left behind and the passion of his work before him.

Six weeks later, on February 12, 1844, the Palestine was in view of the coast of Africa. "With swelling emotions Mr. Campbell retired to his stateroom and returned devoted thanks to Him who had borne him safely o'er the deep in sight of that *dark land,* to which his thoughts and prayers had been devoted for more than eight years."[39]

Arriving in Monrovia, John Milton wrote a letter back to the Mission Board on behalf of himself and Albert Bushnell indicating their safe arrival.

Once in Africa, John could not withhold his passion to share the gospel to any and all who would receive it. "He preached morning and evening to large and attentive audiences."

One evening, however, he returned from worship to find that Rev. William G. Crocker, a fellow passenger on the Palestine and a Baptist missionary, suffering from a hemorrhage of the lungs, perhaps tuberculosis. Thirty-six hours later John led the worship of his colleague's funeral and the moment was so full of the unity of heaven and earth that John exclaimed " I almost desired to accompany brother Crocker thither." In fact, such language of the nearness of death and heaven was much on John's mind, as though he sensed the fragileness of his own life. In an unfinished letter John wrote "bound for Africa and heaven too."[40] John was not alone in such concern for the fragileness of life. The fact was that so many missionaries were dying shortly upon arrival in Africa there was a serious concern of sending missionaries at all, at least those not conditioned to hot tropical conditions. John said he had never felt in such good health.

That was February, 1844. On March 1, John Campbell, Albert Bushnell, and Mrs. Crocker continued south down the coast and four days later landed at Edina to let off Mrs. Crocker at the Baptist Mission. The expedition continued farther south until it reached Cape Palmas, a former Presbyterian Mission that was then run by the Episcopal Church. The mission site was known as Mount Vaughn. For several weeks John enjoyed the best of health as he awaited the ship for the last leg of his journey to the Gaboon Mission Station twelve hundred miles to the East.

On April 10, 1844, John came down with the "African Fever." It seemed at first to be a mild type of the affliction. It wasn't. On April 17 it was apparent he was dying and John knew it. He said calmly, "the will of the Lord be done." He was afraid only that his death added to so many others would only serve to deter others from coming to Africa. His weakness grew and by late evening April 18, John could not respond. He died at 3:00 a.m. on April 19. His body was laid to rest in a grove of palm trees behind the mission house at Mount Vaughn at Cape Palmas.

John Milton Campbell lived life with intensity and urgency. He lived his last days always mindful that death was looking over his shoulder. He was very mindful of the thief in the night. From aboard the ship he wrote the following to his friends and supporters back home, "Should the mighty ocean find me a grave I rejoice that my attention was called to Foreign Missions. Should I soon fall beneath an African climate I trust I shall have no occasion to regret going there either in time or eternity—for I think I have sought unto the Lord and he has directed my steps."[41]

Upon his death a posthumous examination was made and it was determined that rather than the "African Fever" he probably died from complications of the lingering disease of his lungs and heart that caused him to hemorrhage back in Cincinnati.[42] This makes one wonder if he did not have tuberculosis all along. Then again, the issue of sending missionaries to this part of the world was so serious, this addendum diagnosis written as a footnote may have been made more to calm fears for others coming to Africa than offer a complete diagnosis of his condition.

The occasion of John Milton Campbell's death was reason for some to make tribute in verse such as:

Amid the peaceful labors of the field,
Guiding the ploughshare through the furrowed soil,
Or strewing seeds that wake the harvest joy,
Deep thoughts swept over him—thoughts of Afric's need
Benighted and distressed.

And when he bade farewell
To her who lured him—and to him who trained
His happy boyhood, with parental care:
And sought with spreading sail her darkened coast
Who like a brother, weepeth night and day for
Her kidnapped children.

On her care he poured
Salvation's message, with the holy zeal
Of one who only knew the time was short,
A cold hand touched his bosom, and he fell
Faith's quenchless luster in his dying eye,
And on his palid lips the victor's song,
Where Ethiopia tilts her head to God,
Mourning and desolate.[43]

                        Lydia H. Sigourney

Home Forgotten

To Live for Africa; and toil, a hopeful laborer, there,
Thou didst as fearful perils brave, as painful sorrows dare.
Boldly, as if a seraph's hand was pointing out the road,
Thou sever'st life's sweet kindred ties, and gave up all for God.[44]

M.B. Crocker

Fellow missionary Albert Bushnell wrote: "Mr Campbell remarked, just before his death, 'The cause of Christ will go forward; when he takes away one instrument he can raise up others.' "[45]

In the wake of John Campbell's death there was the biography that forged much of this chapter. Thirteen copies of the book are extant in universities around the country. There are the rose windows of the First Presbyterian Church of Ironton and there is one personal artifact handed down by the family in the possession of John Milton Campbell's distant nephew, Dr. Allan C. Campbell, of Peoria, Illinois. Sent home in a small box of John's earthly possessions was the brass candleholder that held the light from which he absorbed the scriptures.

John Milton Campbell's candleholder

There is a sadness that such enthusiasm was cut short of realizing its goal. John Milton Campbell was just a month shy of reaching Gaboon. Yet, he may have in his death been spared an unbearable grief. The Gaboon Mission Station that he lived and breathed to know was not at all what it seemed. It was wrought with problems that were not disclosed to supporting churches back in the United States. In fact, its director, the Rev. John Leighton Wilson of South Carolina, once wrote two letters of the conditions at the mission. One was an optimistic version for the churches. The other was the harsh reality of the situation for the Mission Board to consider and advise.

Competition was keen between Catholic and Presbyterian missions in the area. Each one's worth was determined by the indigenous people more for the food and western goods they could provide than the merit of each church's evangelism. The native peoples listened well to the missionaries that there was a better life, a civilized life that was a part of experiencing the Christian life. Well, the commercial hunters, miners and shippers were better able to provide more commodities of "civilized" life than the Catholics and Presbyterians combined. The missionaries were being ignored by their own values of progress.[46]

John Leighton Wilson freed his numerous slaves before coming to Africa to minister to the Native peoples. As concerned as he was for Africans, he treated black Africans in a condescending spirit and expected them to regard him with elevated respect. Leighton set the tone for dealing with slavery. When the newly-gathered slaves passed by the Mission Station on the way to America, the mission staff was to look the other way. The official position on slavery of the Mission Station and the Mission Board back in America was, "no comment."[47] As we shall see, nothing raised the ire of John Milton Campbell more than slavery. It is hard to imagine that he would have fared well in such a circumstance.

In time the Presbyterian church nurtured an indigenous clergy. The most notable among them was Ntaka Truman. Truman was a bright, enthused convert to the faith and not one to take idly the fact that as a clergy neither he nor any other indigenous pastor was being paid equal to the white missionaries. This finally came to a full boil when Truman demanded to go to America and plead his case before the Mission Board.[48]

There were also issues of American missionaries proselytizing in a French colony. The French did not take kindly to this. At the very time John Campbell was arriving on the African Coast, the French navy was firing its canons on the Gaboon mission determined to drive it away.

By the 1880s the Presbyterians had grown weary of all the dissention, and finding few rewards for their work, eventually withdrew from the Gaboon Station altogether. Mindful of such a legacy, one again notes the grief that John Milton Campbell was spared.[49]

The Mount Vaughn Mission House at Cape Palmas where John Milton Campbell died and is buried.

In fact, the life of John Milton Campbell had an extraordinary impact on his times, more than he himself would ever know. To understand this possibility, we would need to return to his seminary years as he prepared to go to Africa. John's witness to his faith was infectious and in his enthusiasm we find those who found reason in John's life to risk their own lives for a noble and sacred cause. Among them was a fellow student and friend named John Fee.

The friendship of John Milton Campbell and John Fee is central to the next chapter of the book. It brings together the common thread that joins all the chapters of this work and it gives us reason to see how John Milton Campbell's life was fulfilled before he ever left for Africa. Albert Bushell wrote, " ..,perhaps his death may do more for the cause of Christ than many years of life at home would have effected."[50] Certainly his life at home had all ready effected more than anyone imagined.

One hundred sixty years later a check arrives in Alaska. It is a check of mission support from First Presbyterian Church of Ironton, Ohio. The check is addressed to this writer for mission work in Alaska and Russia. It just so happened that the check arrived just in time. A Yupik woman of the Chukotka region of the Russian Far East was heading home. We had provided her with as much help as we could for her battle with cancer. She was heading home for more treatment in Moscow. She was also heading home to be in ministry to her own people who live very meager and humble lives in a terribly austere and isolated world.

Before she left from Nome, Alaska, to Provideniya, Russia, she was given the mission money from the Ironton Church, the church with the windows in honor of John Milton Campbell. She was also told that the money was given in honor of a distant uncle who wanted desperately to care for the people of Africa so many years ago. She was also told the money came from this church in Ohio that was my ancestor's spiritual home. On Monday Morning, September 4, 2006, I received a phone call in broken English. It was Klava Markarova calling from the Nome Airport. She was just about to get on the plane to go home but she needed to talk.

> Jim......Your uncle......Africa......Someday......I will go there for him.

I was pleased, pleased not that she would go to Africa, but that she understood and cared about the story of John Milton Campbell and would share it with her people as she used the mission funds from the Ironton church. I was pleased that after all these years what is remembered is still giving life.

James and Mary had three sons and the life of the eldest was saved to the last because it is through him that this book is brought to the present.

WASHINGTON GREENLEAF CAMPBELL

The eldest son of James W. and Mary Campbell was Washington Campbell, a farmer and a Brown County land appraiser.

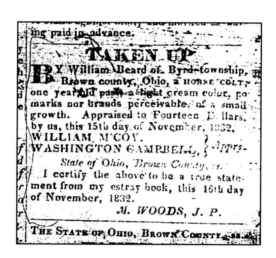

Advertisement for land appraising in the Georgetown Castigator

Washington lived approximately ten miles east of his parents in Byrd Township in the neighborhood of his aunt Sarah Campbell Bimpson, whose sons would eventually help manage the Olive Furnace in Lawrence County and his uncle John W. Campbell, Congressman and U.S. Federal Judge. We know Washington spent some time as a young man at his Uncle John's house because Washington would marry the niece of Uncle John Campbell's wife. Eleanor Jane Lilley and sister Elizabeth went to live with their Uncle John and Aunt Eleanor when their father John Lilley died. Suddenly the two nieces were transported to Ohio from Augusta County, Virginia, and were soon caught up in the life of the political and judicial circles of Columbus, Ohio. They were also introduced to the extended Campbell family that had dispersed around Brown County.

In a letter from John W. Campbell to a Lilley nephew, Uncle John mentions "Of course you heard of the wedding of Washington Campbell to Eleanor Jane." *That was it.* This writer came out of his chair. I wanted to shout through time, "NO! We didn't hear of the wedding of our distant grandfather and grandmother. Don't stop, please don't stop." We were that close to the details, but got no further except to note that Uncle John at least did not say that this marriage of Eleanor Jane to a child of his brother James was a dour affair with somber piety.

We have no account of Washington's relationship to brothers Hiram or John Milton. We know he was industrious, farming an operation requiring two hired hands.[51] He was also, as we shall see, very much caught up in the pressing social issues of his day. Washington would stay in Brown County five years after his father's death. In 1856 Washington moved to Champaign, Illinois.

This move to the west would not be a complete break. Washington and Eleanor's daughter Agnes would marry George Hannah, a druggist from Georgetown, Ohio, and move back to

Brown County. Beyond that were the continued connections to Washington's sisters who stayed behind and to his brother Hiram in Ironton.

It is this last connection that is of special interest. We know from the letter of John Campbell of Ironton to cousin Hiram that John not only wanted Hiram to join him in founding Ironton, but wanted Hiram's mother to come and be a part of this newly emerging city as well. As noted, had Hiram's mother Mary moved east to be with Hiram and his family, she would have had every possible convenience and lived out her aging years in comfort and respect. Mary did not take that option. Instead, at age seventy, Mary chose to go west with son Washington to the frontier life of the prairies of Illinois.

Why did she make that choice? It is a question never answered and one that never goes away.

This chapter ends with one last look at the home place of James W. and Mary Campbell. To family members making pilgrimages to Ohio, there is as much need for pilgrimage to Brown County as there is to Ironton. Here in Brown County are the graves of the ancestors who first crossed the river. William and Elizabeth are buried with some of their children beside the Red Oak Church that was the family's spiritual, social, and as we shall see, moral home.

In Ripley is the First Presbyterian Church attended by Joseph N. Campbell and his sisters. In Ripley is the home where sisters Elizabeth and Edith Campbell were born. Above Ripley is the home of one of the family's pastors, Rev. John Rankin. The Georgetown Church was attended by James and Mary and it is here just outside of Georgetown that the James W. and Mary Campbell farm still stands.

It is from this home that Hiram left to find his fortune in the iron industry. It is from this home that John Milton Campbell left as a missionary to Africa. It was to this home that pioneering grandmother Elizabeth Campbell came to visit as did Uncle John W. on his way back from the U.S. Congress. It was at this home that the Ralston boys would come to visit Grandma. Memories were shared of Grandpa Duncan the frontiersman, visions were contemplated of a new beginning on the Illinois plains, and it was within the walls of this home that the issues of the day played out their course as slaves would make their way north to freedom. Years later, generations later, we would come back. We would stand on hallowed ground and try to imagine, try to honor what once was. We would stand and have our picture taken holding this moment of seeking our heritage. We would try, in passing, to make our way home to something of us, and in us, that until now, we never knew was there.

The home place of James and Mary Campbell on Hillman Ridge

CHAPTER 10

ABOLITION

A hired researcher mentioned it in passing. There was a Campbell family scrapbook from the 1820s at the Cincinnati Historical Society. That brief mention gave cause for the author to take a week off work and fly four thousand miles to Cincinnati in hopes of finding gleanings of personal family memos from the 1820s. The scrapbook was, in fact, pasted newspaper articles in the ledger book of Joseph N. Campbell's mercantile store in Ripley. This ledger gave the store accounts of William and Elizabeth Campbell mentioned briefly in chapter five. The staff of the Cincinnati Historical Society shared my enthusiasm for the find. However, enthusiasm changed to raised eyebrows when the same old ledger revealed, as well, the charge account of Rev. John Rankin, *the* Rev. John Rankin.

To be sure, the ledger did not reveal much other than thirty-five dollars in unspecified charges. Still, that amounted to ten percent of Rankin's annual salary as pastor of Ripley. Serving the Ripley church during very hard times and getting by was a matter of credit held especially by parishioners. Joseph N. Campbell not only carried Rankin on the books but was his chief advocate for missions in the Ripley Church.[1]

All through this research an eye was kept on anything about Rev. John Rankin because it was around him that the book would find the glue that brings the story together. How many times had I had sung the old spiritual "Swing Lo, Sweet Chariot?" I knew the words by heart. Then one day watching a documentary on the Underground Railroad, the richer meaning of the song came through.[2] That spiritual would never be the same. The scene in the documentary was the Ohio River. The Ohio River was the Jordon River in the song. "Home" in the song was Canada and the "band of angels coming after me" were the abolitionists, particularly the abolitionists of Ripley, Ohio. There in the documentary, as "Swing Lo, Sweet Chariot" was sung, appeared Ripley, Ohio. Then the scene changed to the house on the hill, the home of Rev. John Rankin, the pastor of the Presbyterian Church of Ripley.

Mention of Rev. John Rankin's life in the cause of anti-slavery creates with enthusiasts a quick ascent to superlatives. His concern for the freeing of slaves was cause for slave holders to put a high price on his head, dead or alive. Rankin's autobiography indicates these threats were real, full of close calls and intrigue.[3] John Rankin was "the Martin Luther of the Cause" of freedom and in the west, "the father of abolition."[4] Others see Rankin as a more moderate influence on his times, at least compared to the broad visionary work of William Lloyd Garrison.[5] Whatever the slant historians put on Rankin, one could not tell the story of those tumultuous times without including him and the band of followers around him for whom the term "Underground Railroad" first was coined.

When Harriett Beecher Stowe's firestorm book *Uncle Tom's Cabin* was published, the drama of the escape of the slave named Eliza became larger than life when it was revealed that the episode was taken from real life. The one who was central to Eliza's escape was the Rev. John Rankin.

One hundred and fifty years later books are still being written about the life and times of Rev. John Rankin. He is central to defining the making of American identity that would eventually be forged through the Civil War. All the while John Rankin was acting as a local, regional, and national figure of the abolition movement, he was also a pastor of local congregations, with babies to be baptized, couples to be married, and grief to be faced in the death of loved ones. Among the many people who were a part of his parish flock were the children and grandchildren of William and Elizabeth Campbell. One grandchild, John Wilson Humphreys, married the Rankins' daughter Isabella.

Rev. John Rankin

* * * * * * * * * *

There is no record of William or Elizabeth Campbell's attitude toward slavery or the evolution of their conviction, except for the single statement by their grandson Hiram that they left Kentucky to avoid slavery.[6] We remember that William's Grandfather Robert held six slaves in Augusta County at the time of his death in 1768. For that year and for the upper Shenandoah Valley, six slaves were considered a statement of privilege. His father Charles Campbell also had two slaves noted in his will. We do not know whether son William, who inherited the home place, kept the slaves, set them free, or sold them when he immigrated to Kentucky in 1791.

Abolition

What we have is an ethic by association. William and Elizabeth Campbell were members of the Red Oak Church and parishioners of Rev. James Gilliland, who was helping slaves to freedom before the words "Underground Railroad" were ever coined or Rev. John Rankin had arrived. Rev. Gilliland's son would state at the end of the century that support for his father and abolition by the Red Oak congregation was unanimous.[7]

Unanimous support for the cause of anti-slavery did not mean everyone who was anti-slavery was entirely of like mind. There were shades of support and different interpretations as to the best way of doing away with slavery, and those differences between the faithful were also differences within the Campbell home.

* * * * * * * * *

It began in the early 1800s and grew to a fair measure of popular support in the 1820s. It was called colonization. Create a colony in Africa and send the slaves back to the land "from which they came." Those who supported colonization on pragmatic and moral grounds set the plan into motion with the creation of the African nation of Liberia. The process was cumbersome and when set into motion was not met by enthusiasm by most American slaves and freed slaves who were now generations removed from Africa. They wanted freedom in this land of their birth. Furthermore, the cause of colonization was being seen more and more a smoke screen for slave states using it to buy time as they raised a long list of repercussions of what would happen should slavery come abruptly to an end.[8]

The voices of colonization around the country were, if nothing else, forcing the issue of what was the right way to end slavery. Certainly it must have been a hot issue at the Campbell home. The head of the Colonization Society for the state of Ohio was William and Elizabeth's son, Federal Judge John W. Campbell.[9] John's abhorrence of slavery was summarized in a poem he wrote that was the first public expression in the family of disdain for slavery.

My cruel, my inhumane master,
Author of my constant grief,
Brings on me a sore disaster;
Where, now, shall I find relief?

Adieu, dear babies, your father leaves you,
Where you'll never see again;
A savage white man now bereaves you;
We may weep, but all in vain.

He cares not for our lamentation,
He's unjust, and hard his heart;
Because we're of the Afric nation,
Never to meet we must now depart.

Your mother's gone: she dwells in heaven;
There she sings immortal praise;
But to Florida I'm driven,
There to spend my wretched days.

Are we brutes? Have we no reason,
That we thus are bought and sold—
That we thus must, every season,
Still accumulate their gold?[10]

Such heartfelt loathing of the institution of slavery was in tension with John's pragmatic spirit of compromise and moderation in all things. In the U.S. Congress John was a champion of the middle ground, which is why he was a candidate for U.S. Speaker of the House. Colonization seemed a common ground between North and South by making the slavery problem, eventually, just go away. It also was the only common ground he could hold between his own personal beliefs and political realities. Jacksonian Democrats were not about to rock the boat over slavery. If colonization was a way to advocate against slavery and still maintain party loyalty, John not only chose this route but became the state chairman of the Colonization Society.

Then there was home.

With an empty house from the death of both of their adopted children, John W. and Eleanor entertained the idea of the guardianship of two teenaged daughters of the late John Lilley, husband of Eleanor's sister. As noted, in 1825 Elizabeth and Eleanor Jane Lilley left their home in Greeneville, Virginia, for "Uncle Campbell's" farm out west at Russellville in Brown County, Ohio.

Such a move was not only traumatic in leaving extended family after the death of their parents, it was also a move into quite a different world that was at the very heart of the controversy over slavery. Slavery for both Lilley sisters was a way of life. In fact, both sisters were owners of two slaves named Anderson and Mary. Well, at least they owned a percentage of the two slaves—and the sisters were not willing to yield their shares in the slaves to their frustrated older brother.[11] Perhaps it was a maneuver to keep the two slaves from being sold. Neither sister gave in for some time.

Introduction to life in Brown County meant introduction to the rest of the Campbell family and their pastors Rev. Rankin and Rev. Gilliland. For the two Lilley sisters the gospel is now expressed as abolition and witnessing to the freeing of slaves through the Red Oak Church where they worshiped. All the while there were letters from back home in Virginia mentioning such things as cousin Gabriel Lilley moving to Warren County, Kentucky, keeping ten slaves, five men, two women and three children, "just enough to maintain a comfortable life."[12] Eventually brother William Lilley joined his sisters in Brown

County working for Uncle Campbell. A letter from William expresses the deep concern of many folks he finds and affirms in Ohio, who are worried about the Indian uprisings in Illinois. With so many white men off to fight the Indian Wars, would the vacuum at home encourage an uprising of the slaves?[13]

In the midst of the commotion between the forces of pro-slavery and anti-slavery, Uncle John's brother James W. decides he has had enough of a slavery society in Kentucky and finally moves in 1825 with his family of grown or near-grown children to join the rest of the Campbells in Brown County, Ohio. James W.'s move gives reason to intensify the family's resolve against slavery. The move, we remember, also introduces Eleanor Jane Lilley to Washington Campbell, the oldest son of James W.

One wonders about the romance that follows between abolitionist Washington Campbell, who would join the Ripley Anti-slavery Society[14] and Eleanor Jane Lilley, who did not join the Anti-slavery Society. Eleanor Jane still held part ownership in two slaves in Virginia and that must have made for an interesting courtship.

Everything was so complicated and the feelings so intense. The James W. Campbell family had a shared bond of upholding abolitionist principles. Son John Milton Campbell went to Lane Theological Seminary in preparation for missionary work in Africa. His tenure at Lane was after the famed uprising of the Lane Rebels who brought the seminary to a standstill in their promotion of abolitionist principles. John M. Campbell was very much a part of that lingering rebel spirit. At one debate at Lane he joined the side of advocates who professed that no person owning a slave should be given the sacrament of Holy Communion.[15]

John wrote to his brother Hiram to see if Hiram was yet affirming the family values of abolition. Hiram had married and moved back to Kentucky to work for his wife's uncle in the iron industry. Hiram not only affirmed abolition but trumped his brother's conviction by saying the freedom of the slaves should be immediate and complete. John M. Campbell was firm in his conviction of abolition but wasn't so sure of the word, "immediate."[16]

In fact, we later learn that brother Hiram had not held to the family principles as he had said. Hiram's employment at the ironworks in Kentucky put him in charge of managing one hundred slaves—and when the day was over, Hiram had ownership of a slave to keep his home.[17] The temptation to slavery was very real. One wonders if this contradiction of principle may have been at least part of the reason that Hiram became disenchanted with his introduction to the iron industry. One also wonders what it was like for Hiram to come home to Brown County living the secret of his owning a slave in the continued abolition witness of the family and the sacrifices of Rev. Rankin for the cause.

In 1836 Hiram left Kentucky to join cousin John C. Campbell in managing the Mount Vernon Iron Furnace in Lawrence County, Ohio. When he joined cousin John it was not just for producing iron. Cousin John was quietly helping freed slaves of the region, offering safe houses and passage north to freedom. In a matter of days, Hiram went from slave owner to a participant of what would be the Underground Railroad. At first Hiram only offered assistance as he was asked.[18] Later in Ironton, he and his household became major participants in the movement. One wonders if among the many he would help to freedom included those Hiram once managed or owned in Kentucky.

All of this serves to underline how complicated the issue of slavery was not only in the diverse passions in Brown County but also within the anti-slavery circles and churches. Life was not a clean cut either-or. It was a struggle that extended into the most ardent abolitionist families and finally into the internal conflicts of the conscience of individuals. In the late 1840s James W. Campbell, a founding trustee of the Georgetown Presbyterian Church, transferred his membership from the Georgetown to the Red Oak church of his parents ten miles to the southeast. That would not be all that unusual except that Mary Duncan Campbell, his wife, kept her membership at Georgetown. For a husband and wife to maintain memberships in separate churches gives cause to wonder. A close look suggests that James responded to the internal tensions over slavery of the Georgetown Church. Eventually these tensions tore the church apart into two separate congregations. Mary stayed with the struggle in Georgetown. James responded by removing to the Red Oak church, the family's home church that had always been of like mind against slavery.

When the Anti-slavery Society of Ripley was formed in 1835 the only Campbell name on the roster of this family line was Washington Campbell. Washington was one among five others around the immediate vicinity of the Red Oak Church that was ready to "feed, secrete and forward the fugitives."[19] Washington was an exception in the county in his willingness to hire a freed slave from Virginia by the name of Nicholas Highwarden. [20]

The absence of other Campbells on the Anti-slavery Society roster is deceiving. Joseph and John, sons of William and Elizabeth, had already died. Son Charles had moved to Illinois. Washington's brothers had moved away. It was the daughters who show up on the roster. Daughter Elizabeth Campbell married William Humphreys and both were members of the Ripley Anti-slavery Society. Sister Rebecca Campbell married William Baird. They not only were members of the society but maintained one of the known "refuges" in the Ripley area for fleeing slaves. Sister Fidelia Campbell, a member of the Anti-slavery Society, married Benjamin Hopkins whose family was instrumental in the story of rescuing Eliza's children that was a dominant image in Harriet Beecher Stowe's *Uncle Tom's Cabin*.[21]

Besides these was the known commitment to abolition and the providing of refuge by William B. Campbell, son of Joseph N. Campbell who died in 1833. William B. married Mary Leavitt whose Ripley Family also ran one of the refuges for slaves.[22]

Finally, there was elder brother, James W. Campbell who left Kentucky to avoid slavery and whose family bond was a vow against slavery. We don't know why James and wife Mary Duncan Campbell didn't join the Anti-slavery Society as did his son Washington and James' sisters. What we do know of James and Mary is seen through the eyes of their children, especially son John Milton Campbell who attributed the moral character of his life to the nurturing of his mother and father. Surely, if son John Milton Campbell had not been away to school he would have been more than a part of the anti-slavery movement in Brown County. At every chance John loved to witness to what he believed. With that we note that John had a special gift in addressing slavery that warranted the attention and respect of even slaveholders. Wrote John M. Campbell's biographer:

> *Against American slavery he [John Milton Campbell] was ever accustomed to protest it as an "accursed thing" and he labored against it in a way that doubtless promises the most certain and speedy success.... in his intercourse with slaveholders, which was not inconsiderable, he was accustomed to reason with them in regard to the sinfulness of their course, with great plainness, yet in a calm and affectionate manner, so that those very slaveholders would afterwards entertain feelings of respect and friendship towards him; for however little effect his reasoning might produce on their minds, they could not but feel that his were the words of a sincere and conscientious man. Instances*

might be cited of his being cheerfully and hospitably entertained by those whom he repeatedly reproved for the sin of slaveholding.[23]

Certainly such a healing voice in a world of strident shouts would have been reason enough to remember this young man. A week after ordination he was off to Africa as a missionary and, as we have noted, for that and his world map of missions he will be remembered. But he should be remembered for more, something he himself would never live to see.

John Milton Campbell graduated from Miami University of Ohio in 1840 and that same year entered the beginning class at Lane Theological Seminary. In seminary John M. not only devoted himself to his theological studies and his added studies of medicine two miles away, but he was also filling any extra moment with lecturing on missions to churches in the region and aiding in the mission outreach to Native American tribes in Indiana.

As noted, all this effort cost John his health. In addition to all his professional activities, he was also very much involved with the lives of his classmates, which brings us to his relationship with fellow student John G. Fee.

John Fee was a Methodist theological student from Kentucky. He was a classmate of John's at Miami University and later at Lane seminary. They were good friends and in that friendship found reason to address the institution of slavery. This to John Fee was much more than an academic dialogue. John Fee came from a home that not only had slaves but were strongly fixed in the advocacy of slavery. What follows is the account of the encounters of John Fee and John M. Campbell at Lane Theological Seminary taken from John Fee's autobiography.

I entered Lane Seminary in the year 1842. Here I met in class one of my former classmates, John Milton Campbell, a former student at Oxford, Ohio. He was a man of marked piety and great goodness of heart. Years previously he had consecrated himself to the work of missions and chose West Africa as his field. Another member of the same class was James C. White, formerly of Boston, Massachusetts, late pastor of the Presbyterian church on Poplar St., Cincinnati. These brethren became deeply interested in me as a native of Kentucky and in view of my relation to the slave system, my father being a slaveholder. They pressed upon my conscience the text, 'Thou shalt love the Lord thy God with all thy heart, and thy neighbor as thy self,' and as a practical manifestation of this, 'Do unto men as ye would they should do unto you.' I saw that the duty enjoined was fundamental in the religion of Jesus Christ, and that unless I embraced the principle and lived it in honest practice, I would lose my soul. I saw also that as an honest man I ought to be willing to wear the name which would be a fair exponent of the principle I espoused. This was the name Abolitionist, odious then to the vast majority of people North, and especially South. I saw that to embrace the principle and wear the name was to cut myself off from relatives and former friends, and apparently from all prospects of usefulness in the world. I had in the grove near the seminary a place to which I went every day for prayer, between the hours of eleven and twelve. I saw that to have light and peace from God, I must make the consecration. I said, 'Lord, if needs be, make me an Abolitionist.' The surrender was complete. I arose from my knees with the consciousness that I had died to the world and accepted Christ in all the fullness of his character as I then understood Him.

Soon after the submission and consecration referred to, the question arose, Where ought I to expend my future efforts, and manifest forth this love to God and man? ...I was considering seriously the duty of going with J. M. Campbell, my classmate, to Western Africa; and was in correspondence with the American Board of Commissioners for Foreign Missions in reference to my going as a missionary abroad.

Whilst these fields of labor were being considered, there came irresistibly the consideration of another field: that part of the home field which lay in the South, and especially in Kentucky, my native State.[24]

The Rev. John G. Fee

John G. Fee would go on to become the most noted abolitionist in the state of Kentucky. He was disowned by his family and ran huge risks of harboring fugitive slaves as they made their way through Kentucky to Ohio. Later he would help start a school that became Berea College in Berea, Kentucky. Victor B. Howard's book, *The Evangelical War Against Slavery and Caste: The Life and Times of John G. Fee,* promoted his work with the words, "John G. Fee is a unique and rare figure in the antislavery movement, and he became the most important and influential reformer to wage war against slavery in the South."[25]

Abolition

Today Berea College is a living witness to the work and vision of Rev. John Fee. At the same time the school is, through John Fee, a memorial to a man whose influence changed the course of Fee's life in dedication to abolition and almost persuaded him to mission work in Africa. In the end, the relationship between these two seminarians may have been one of the most profound legacies of John Milton Campbell's life. If John Milton Campbell was so gifted in his anti-slavery witness as to command respect from slave owners, even if they were not moved to change, then there was an exception. One did listen and change—Rev. John Fee of Kentucky.

That exception is to be noted and celebrated as not only a part of John M. Campbell's life but the legacy of Brown County. The story of a people is not just what happens and is remembered between them but what extends from them. A closer look at the argument John Campbell used to persuade John Fee, the argument that was so compelling and remembered late into Fee's life, "Who is your neighbor?".... was most certainly borrowed directly from Rev. John Rankin. These words of John Campbell's argument, almost word for word, were what Rankin himself considered his prime argument against slavery.[26] The impressions received from Rev. John Rankin lived through his parishioner to harvests neither realized in one who would become Kentucky's most ardent spirit of anti-slavery.

* * * * * * * * * *

Grandmother Elizabeth Wilson Campbell died in 1832. That was also the year her grandson John C. Campbell began to make his way in the world in the iron industry. Within four years John had risen from a bookkeeper to part owner of Campbell, Ellison and Company and its Mt. Vernon Furnace in Lawrence County, Ohio. It was here, as previously noted, that at least by 1836 John and now cousin Hiram were already aiding the efforts of slaves fleeing from Virginia and Kentucky.

In 1848, John Campbell was ready to make his move to establish the town of Ironton. As noted, the great commercial center he foresaw and proclaimed for Hanging Rock two years earlier didn't happen. His hands were tied. This time it would happen just up river to the east of Hanging Rock. It would be called Ironton.

As John Campbell was setting his vision into motion for Ironton, the election year of 1847-48 began to unfold. In that election neither national party was addressing the issue of slavery. It was an issue too hot to handle. A ground swell arose for a third party, the anti-slavery party, the Free Soil Party. Its stand against slavery caused John not only to support the Free Soil Party but be a representative to its national convention in Buffalo, New York. John's vision for a commerce center for the iron industry was put on hold. The issue of slavery held the moment.

The sudden immersion into the politics of the Free Soil Party makes us wonder who in this movement caught John Campbell's eye and imagination. It is doubtful that it was the party's selection for president, Martin Van Buren. Van Buren's dedication to the cause of anti-slavery was nominal and he got the nomination from the political clout of the Northeast. It certainly was not the vice-presidential candidate Charles F. Adams who had no passion at all and was not the favorite candidate of the party. No, the most popular man for vice-president, indeed in the party, declined to run. The man who most embodied the spirit of the Free Soil Party and demonstrated the ability to create a coalition of a variety of anti-slavery groups stood at the sidelines. His name was Marcus Morton, twice governor of Massachusetts.[27]

All of this has meaning only because a year and a half after the election, hundreds of miles west of Ironton, another town was being formed. John Campbell's brother James M.

Abolition

had platted the streets and younger brother Joseph Harvey Campbell named the town "Morton"....for Marcus Morton of Massachusetts.[28]

As noted earlier, the naming of an Illinois town for a Massachusetts governor seems so untenable that people reach for alternatives that seem just as unlikely. Perhaps the town of Morton was named for the one man of the Free Soil movement that, for a moment in time, caught the eye of their brother John Campbell, who was a delegate to the National Free Soil Anti-Slavery convention in Buffalo. It may be that Morton, Illinois, is named not just for a man, but a moment in time, when a grassroots uprising of anti-slavery spirit had its day.

Then again, maybe Morton was the maiden name for the woman who was the best cook in town.

* * * * * * * * *

The founding of Ironton happened a year later in 1849. As the first surveys were being laid out for Ironton, John Campbell, as stressed earlier in this work, sought out family. The Brown County connection beckoned family members to their cousin's vision and good fortune. Key among them, again, was cousin Hiram Campbell who was managing the Mount Vernon Furnace. As the town of Ironton unfolded, the two cousins who now had worked together fourteen years built two large manor homes that sit side by side. Both homes were places of refuge for fleeing slaves.

John Campbell had a special room built of brick on the roof which makes a heavy load on the weight-bearing walls. Slaves would enter from an inconspicuous door on the third floor with wooden stairs to the roof sanctuary. Because of the roof's facade around the edges, it was not possible to see the secret room from the street. From the street, however, both John and Hiram's homes stood out as bold, obvious statements of prosperity. They seemed the least likely refuge for those who, hours before had been hiding in the woods on the south side of the river.

Today the John Campbell Home is on the National Historical Register and is used by the social service agencies of Ironton for their offices. It is possible to still enter the "secret room" of John Campbell's home. Its dark, dust-laden interior beckons one's imagination to what once happened here. One ascends the steep stairs from the third floor and stands in the dim glow of a bare light bulb, trying to imagine the hope and fear once concentrated in this small space. What really catches the eye are the stairs, the wooden stairs leading up into the darkness. It is the wear that catches the eye. These stairs were not for occasional use. They are worn stairs. It is the wear of these stairs that is the true glory of this old mansion.

The home and Underground Railroad station of John Campbell

Before we go further, it is important to underline the serious concern of Professor Keith Griffler's work, *Frontline of Freedom*.[29] The Underground Railroad was America's first interracial liberation movement, a movement in which white and black operatives played their part and together accomplished a significant influence not only in ushering slaves to freedom but bringing an end to slavery itself. For well over a hundred years a stereotype image has emerged of the fleeing passive slaves being helped to freedom at the mercy of white abolitionists. In truth, the fleeing slaves were not passive. Many, if not most, of the operatives that facilitated escape were freed slaves or free-born blacks who stood the severest consequences (beyond the risks of their white accomplices) if they were caught. The story of the Underground Railroad in Ripley, Ohio, could not be told without serious attention given not only to the primary heroic witness of freed slave John P. Parker but the many other freed slaves who, with Parker, were in fact what Professor Griffler called the *Frontline of Freedom*.

In like manner, the story of the organization of the Underground Railroad before Ironton was formed was a story with roots back to early black settlers in Lawrence County whom John and Hiram Campbell and other white abolitionists helped. As the movement became more defined, the organizational intrigue and ingenuity of the Underground Railroad centered around freed slaves Gabriel Johnson, a barber in Ironton, and Joseph Ditcher whose many incredible risks and near captures over and over earned him the title "The Red Fox." They too were but the most noted of a whole network of black and white participants in the liberation of slaves to freedom.[30]

From those black and white persons who orchestrated and facilitated the flight of slaves north, the immediate goal was most often, though not always, to get the slaves to the black community of Poke Patch to the north in Gallia County. More commonly, the escape would begin at the Ohio River crossing at Hanging Rock. The hushed password for fleeing slaves along the Ohio was "menare" which means "to flow" or "to move with the water." On either side of the river there was a password from safe house to safe house. The most common password phrase to accompany the knock at the door was "a friend of a friend." Along the routes that led to Ironton, however, there was a variation. The knock at the door was accompanied with the words, "handle with tongs."[31] One wonders if the metaphor of these words was not borrowed from the language of the iron furnaces as they used tongs to bring iron out of the fire.

If there was a direct route heading to Ironton, then to Olive Furnace, nineteen miles north, such a direct line was complemented with a weave of options including Mount Vernon, Buckhorn, and other iron furnaces. These options were essential not only to throw off the slave hunters on constant prowl but to mind the eye of the regional federal marshall who had to enforce the fugitive slave law. He was headquartered in Ironton.

Before heading north some fleeing slaves would stay with Gabe Johnson or hide at the Campbell homes or other safe houses. The key, then, was effective transportation north. John Campbell was the main facilitator of this travel. East from the John Campbell home is the First Presbyterian Church, one block south of the church was John's old barn.

Here horses were ready to go in a moment's notice, often used by Rev. Joseph Chester, pastor of the Presbyterian Church who was a constant "conductor" of and chief advocate of the abolition cause. Sometimes as many as fifteen fleeing slaves were waiting in the barn for passage north. John Campbell kept a large covered wagon in the barn pulled by four horses and driven by Gabe Johnson just for these purposes.[32]

There remain many harrowing accounts of the hundreds of slaves that passed through this region to freedom. In them John Campbell was referred by former slaves as "the friend of the black man."[33] That tribute was most evident at his funeral attended by scores of black mourners.

The *Ironton Register*, records:

> *He was a friend of the unfortunate. No wonder the colored people flocked to his funeral, and tearfully viewed him for the last time. He was their friend in the dark days of slavery, no fugitive ever came to this town, searching for freedom, but that Mr. Campbell took his hand, gave him money and sent him on. His home was the asylum for the oppressed in those days.*[34]

The work of John Campbell may have been more than local and regional activism. Professor Griffler notes that as John Campbell worked in tandem with the strategies and heroics of black abolitionists at the Ohio River and those at Poke Patch, he was also working in tandem with the "Order of the Twelve"[35] that was based in St. Louis and led by the famed Moses Dickson. On the surface the Order of the Twelve was but one of several black fraternal organizations helping freed slaves gain a foothold in starting a new life and finding community. Bound together by Masonic Lodge rituals, the Order of the Twelve, however, was not only helping freed slaves but actively facilitating and affording communication between communities of the Underground Railroad. After the Civil War the work of the Order of the Twelve continued in developing numerous chapters of its fraternal organizations that encouraged social development and identity in black communities. One of the strongest and long-lasting chapters was in Ironton, Ohio.

C. Robert Leith's work *Follow The Furnaces*,[36] mentions twice the influence of Rev. John Rankin on John Campbell's life. Leith's connection of Rankin to John Campbell was underscored by others, including a comment from freed slave Catherine Cummings. This is very important. Rankin was what John absorbed from values expressed to values set into action. Rankin's witness became a transplanted spirit into Lawrence County with an Underground Railroad that was as daring, organized, and motivated by blacks and whites "in tandem" as any along the river.

All this has special meaning to the larger picture of the influence of Rev. John Rankin. At Ripley, Ohio, one can tour the national landmark of the Rankin home and consider some of the local places of refuge still standing including the Red Oak Church. Beyond the immediate vicinity there are churches reaching to the north that were founded by Rev. Rankin. The reach goes even further to Zanesville where John Rankin formed and held the first Ohio Anti-Slavery Society meeting. Then there are all the places across the land where Rankin spoke on behalf of abolition, suggesting the larger stage of influence that contributed to Rankin's national recognition.

And yet, the further one goes from Ripley and Brown County the more the larger picture of the work of Rev. John Rankin and the Ripley Anti-slavery Society begins to blur—one exception being in Lawrence County. It is to Ironton that so many of Rankin's parishioners from Brown County migrated to work in the iron industry. It was here that Rankin's moral grounding against slavery was dramatically realized in John and Hiram Campbell. It was here in Lawrence County at the age of eighty that Rev. John Rankin came to visit his granddaughter, who as mentioned in an earlier chapter was also the great-granddaughter of William and Elizabeth Campbell and second cousin to John Campbell. The Rankins stayed long enough in Lawrence County for John to write his autobiography.[37] At the same time Rankin turned his family visit into active ministry. John Rankin preached in Ironton in the morning then rode seven miles to Sheridan to preach in the afternoon. He then returned for the evening services at the First Presbyterian Church in Ironton. Then, John Rankin "went to bed and rested as comfortably as if [he] had performed no labor, and no blue Monday followed. Such is the strength the Lord has given me after being over eighty years of age."[38]

Abolition

With this statement Rankin's autobiography ends. He and his wife live for a while in Kansas where she would die in 1878. In 1881 John Rankin returns to Ironton to live out his days not only with his granddaughter, who had moved from Brown County, but all the other Brown County transplants as well.

When John Rankin died in 1886, his body lay in state in the bay window of his granddaughter's home. "Irontonians of all races and religions walked past the window to pay their respects."[39] Every clergy in Ironton was present at the funeral. Among the pallbearers carrying his casket was one who had also carried his cause, John Campbell.[40]

Twenty-six years later, Monday, September 23, 1912, a grand parade filled the main street of Ironton. Now aged slaves who had been freed for fifty years marched in celebration of "Emancipation Day." It was called "the greatest holiday of the calendar" for black Americans. Amidst all of the cheer in the echo of the word *freedom* came a quiet moment, "one which carried with it a note of deep sentiment" as flowers were placed on the lawn of the home where John Rankin lived his last days.[41] Seven blocks west of these flowers were the worn steps to the dark attic of John Campbell's home; stairs silent, reminders of another time and the influence of Rev. John Rankin on a young parishioner who moved away.

Today, the home where John Rankin died still bears his tribute. It is the museum of the Lawrence County Historical Society. Its presence bears testimony that the life of John Rankin is told not only in where he lived most of his life but also in the meaning and influence of his life on the town in which he died.

Home Forgotten

Rev. John Rankin's last home
Lawrence County Historical Society

* * * * * * * * * *

Two hundred miles northwest of Ironton is Christ Hospital in Cincinnati and the portrait of Dr. Elizabeth Campbell, medical pioneer, the first woman physician to practice in Cincinnati. There is also the Elizabeth Campbell Women's Clinic. Not too far away, in tribute to her sister, is the technical school that once was M. Edith Campbell Junior High. On Auburn Street is the Campbell sisters' home that is a part of a walking tour of historic Cincinnati. We have covered all of this. We have outlined the incredible firsts of these two sisters who were the great-granddaughters of William and Elizabeth Campbell. What we have not noted in the narrative of these accomplishments is that both sisters took the greatest pride in stating over and over that they saw their lives as an extension of the abolitionist spirit of their parents and grandparents in Ripley, Ohio. Their family heritage lived in them and inspired them with a passionate social conscience. From their family's past they drew inspiration to address issues of social justice for the living of their days, extending the values of their ancestors into the twentieth century.

When Edith Campbell was granted an honorary doctor of humanities degree from the University of Cincinnati in 1931, the *Cincinnati-Times Star* stated, "Miss Campbell has long been interested in the Woman's Trade Union League and in the work of labor organizations. Since her childhood days, under the influence of her father, who was a prominent abolitionist, she has been keenly interested in inter-racial problems, and helped to organize the Negro Civic Welfare Association in Cincinnati of which she has served as a board member for many years."[42]

When sister Elizabeth Campbell received national recognition as one of "six social hygiene pioneers" from the American Social Hygiene Association, her award bore witness that she came from "a family who had already established a record for faithful public service."[43] Mostly, however, Elizabeth referred to her mother's side of the family.

If their abolitionist father William B. Campbell was a role model and inspiration to sister Edith in race relations, he was a thorn always remembered, if forgiven, by Elizabeth. While still forging ahead as "a medical crusader" at age eighty-one, the *Cincinnati Enquirer* notes, "Her forebears were staunch abolitionists, their home was a part of the "underground" system for escape of slaves. But Elizabeth's father for a long time strongly opposed her growing desire to be a doctor."[44]

The statement is telling. It bears a disappointment that Elizabeth's father could stand for the freedom of slaves but he would not stand for the freedom of his daughter to be what she chose. Such an observation is critical to understanding how the Campbell sisters saw the gift of heritage. Abolition and all of the risks of the Underground Railroad was not to be an isolated expression of justice. It was not a badge of prestige to be worn by one generation to celebrate the previous generation's vision. To the Campbell sisters one form of justice should set the stage for another. A stand on anti-slavery becomes reason to stand against any form of oppression. Where Elizabeth and Edith took the spirit of their Brown County ancestors is also a part of the story of their Brown County ancestors. Abolition was not just an epoch in time of what once happened in Brown County, but where it led.

* * * * * * * * *

Through the witness of Rev. John Milton Campbell, the anti-slavery community of Brown County influenced the work of John Fee. In John C. and Hiram Campbell, the seeds of this same community found the most fertile new ground in Lawrence County. In Elizabeth and Edith Campbell that same spirit found new direction in social justice in Cincinnati. Finally, abolitionist Washington Campbell would move to Champaign, Illinois, where he would set aside the summer kitchen for housing fleeing slaves, just as he had done before on his farm near the Red Oak Church in Brown County.

All of this together is a part of the story of abolition. It is a part of the history of Brown County. It is the story of those who left, those who moved on and yet brought with them the values and connections of home.

CHAPTER 11
NOTABLE EXCEPTIONS

*William Campbell   Elizabeth Wilson Campbell
James, Charles, John W., Joseph N., Elizabeth, Mary, Rebecca,
Samuel,* **Phoebe***, Sarah, Fidelia*

The Campbells of the North River migrated to the Ohio Valley and then scattered to the winds. Well, not quite. There was an exception, a child of William and Elizabeth whose descendants not only continued to stay in Brown County but live there to this day.

*Mary Martin Bick of Ripley, Ohio.
Her family is the last of the Campbells living in Brown County*

Their ninth child, Phoebe, was born in 1795 in Kentucky and married Henry Martin on June 4, 1818. In fact, Henry was much the "boy next door" with the Martins living just down the road. The original Martin homestead still stands as does the home that Henry built for his large family.

The home built by Henry and Phoebe Campbell Martin

Phoebe bore nine children: Alexander, William, Elizabeth, John, Henry, Jane, Harriet, Samuel, and Mary. A closer look at the names reveal their Campbell ties. The first son, Alexander, was named for grandfather Martin. The middle name for Alexander was Wilson as in Elizabeth Wilson Campbell, his grandmother. The second child, Elizabeth Martin, also honored grandmother Campbell. The third child, William Campbell Martin, born in 1824 was named for his grandfather Campbell who had died two years earlier. William would live to the age of twenty. His untimely death in Tennessee caused his father to bring the body home for burial among the family. Note that on the tombstone honor is given to his Campbell roots with his full name spelled out.

Tombstone of William Campbell Martin

Phoebe Campbell Martin built her life around her nine children. That's how they remember her. Phoebe's granddaughter, Jennie Martin, wrote that her grandmother "was modest and meek. She was the most amiable woman and well beloved by all who knew her. Her devoted Christian life had great influence upon her family and my father loved to dwell on her piety. Unknown to fame she was content to live a sequestered life, faithfully to perform the duties of wife and mother. She was one of whom it was written, 'her children shall rise up and call her blessed.' "[1]

Jennie Martin was the daughter of Phoebe and Henry's fourth child John Martin. John Martin was eighteen years old when his first cousin John Milton Campbell was ordained into the ministry in Ripley with a calling to Africa. One wonders if younger cousin John Martin was present at the ordination or even if both Johns may have been named for the same uncle. John Martin sought first to be a lawyer. He was admitted to the Ohio bar and practiced law until his calling to the ministry. Like his cousin, John Martin graduated from Lane Theological Seminary. Also like his cousin, he was given to missions; only instead of Africa, John Martin answered the call to home missions and the rigors of the American frontier. In the fall of 1880 John Martin and his family moved to Silver Ridge, Nebraska. There he left his family in more civil surroundings as he made his way to the more remote community of St. Edwards one hundred miles away.

Life in the early development of Nebraska was harsh. At times, the stresses on John and his family gave temptation to leave. John persisted until the end of his life and became a much-beloved presence in the forming of the Presbyterian Church of Nebraska.

Rev. John Martin
son of Henry and Phoebe Campbell Martin

Notable Exceptions

If John Milton Campbell was defined by his heroic singularity of vision, his passion, his outspoken resolve to go at all costs to proclaim the gospel to the ends of the earth, cousin John Martin was equally given to a witness of peace and quiet compassion.

To read the biographical essays of John Martin's life by his daughter and others who knew and loved him, is to be taken by a witness of an extraordinarily kind and gentle human being. He was a man so in contrast to the raw, coarse and sometimes brutal mission environment he served. "He was a man who loved peace," wrote his granddaughter. Colleague Rev. William Kimball stated, "To the poor and unfortunate he gave special attention, and ministered to them not only in spiritual things, but in material things, carrying food to the hungry, preparing kindling wood for the widow's winter fire, and other similar acts of benevolence which made him dearly beloved by the people."[2]

These words were not just the sentiments reserved for something to say in a funeral eulogy. Humaneness truly was the man, not only to others but to all of God's creatures.

Judge J. C. Robinson put flesh on what that meant. Robinson noted that even when John Martin was physically weak, he would get out of the buggy and walk up the hill to lessen the burden of his horse. Robinson then told of a farmer who was "driving a team of horses hitched to a loaded wagon along the street near their home, when one of the horses stepped into a hoop and fell. The driver began to whip the horse to make it rise, and just then Mr. Martin came running toward him and called out in a loud voice, 'Stop striking that horse! Stop striking that horse or I'll have you arrested!' The man stopped whipping the horse, and Mr. Martin assisted him in releasing the animal and getting him up, and in a kindly way, gave him good advice on the treatment of his horses; the farmer thanked him, and the men separated better friends than when they met."[3]

It is now one hundred and twenty years since John Martin's death. There is no Presbyterian Church in Hartington, Nebraska. John Martin and his wife Sarah are buried in the local cemetery and locals are not familiar with the name. They are not even aware that there once was a Presbyterian Church, let alone a Presbyterian minister who knew and cared for nearly everyone in Cedar County. He and Sarah are forgotten but to God. No one in Huntington can find their graves. Still, the little book about John Martin's life has remained and the depth of character and faith it portrays is timeless. The witness of such a kind and gentle human being in the face of hard, hard times and a frontier spirit, still gives life, wonder and thanksgiving. It also gives reason for him to be remembered in these pages of his ancestors.

* * * * * * * * *

Notable Exceptions

The second exception in this book concerns the premise that the Campbells of the North River who settled in Brown County were William, Elizabeth, and their eleven children. There was one more Campbell in Brown County with roots to the North River. That Campbell was Charles Fenelon Campbell, a grand-nephew of William Campbell, the grandson of William's older brother Charles, which brings us back to the legacy of all the Charles diagramed in chapter one.

<u>The Legacies of Charles</u>

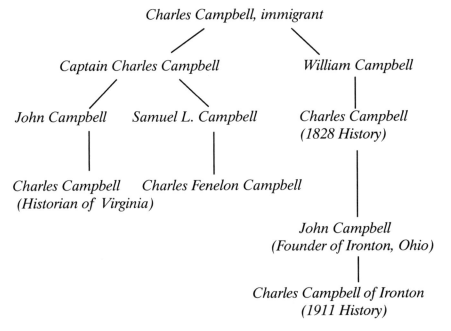

Charles F. Campbell's father, Dr. Samuel Legrand Campbell, was a physician in Rockbridge County, Virginia, as well as the president of Washington College from 1797 to 1799 that became Washington and Lee University.

Samuel's youngest son, Charles F. Campbell was admitted to the bar after receiving a degree from Washington College. He moved to Ripley in 1823, a year after his great-uncle William's death. At first Charles taught school and served as a justice of the peace. He later became a probate judge, mayor of the town of Ripley, and eventually a member of the Ohio State Senate. From 1842 to 1845 Charles was a prosecuting attorney for Brown County. Because Charles had military experience, he was responsible for the training of the first troops of the Ripley area for the Civil War.

Charles was the editor of *The Ohio Whig* in 1840 and the *Ripley Bee* from 1849 to 1862. The *Ripley Bee* would later look back on its former editor and note that Charles Campbell "was an educated and generous citizen, an able lawyer, and left a reputation for honesty and ability that is a grand inheritance of his family."[4]

In 1833, Charles Campbell married Harriet Kephart. Both Charles and Harriet were members of the Ripley Anti-slavery Society and attended the Ripley Presbyterian Church with their distant Campbell cousins. To Charles and Harriet were born one daughter and five sons. All five sons served in the Civil War and all five of them would become newspaper editors in Iowa and Ohio.

Son Agnus K. was the editor of the *Jasper Free Press* in Newton, Iowa, and was also involved in manufacturing. He invented the factory heating system process that became the standard of industrial factory heating. His brother, Frank T. Campbell, also edited the *Jasper Free Press* and from there the Montezuma, Iowa, *Republican*. Frank went on to serve in the Iowa senate and became, for a term, the Lieutenant Governor of Iowa. Brother William A. Campbell became editor of the Lima, Ohio, *Republican Gazette* and its follow up the Lima *Gazette*. Brothers John Q. A. and Charles Campbell became editors of the Bellefontaine, Ohio, *Republican*.

Notable Exceptions

In May of 1906 all five sons and daughter Nettie Christie joined their aged mother for a grand family reunion in Ripley. It was of such note as to garner the front page of the *Ripley Bee*.

Ripley Bee, May 16, 1906

CHAPTER 12

HOME FORGOTTEN

Everything in this book up to this chapter was lost. All of it, save only the minor exception that the Campbell family that moved on to Illinois handed on to its children that it migrated from Ripley, Ohio, and before that Flemingsburg, Kentucky. There was an uncle who was a missionary and an uncle named "Ross" who died in Andersonville Prison. That was it— a family legacy in two sentences. All too soon the Ohio connections became vague and disconnected.

The disconnection went in both directions. It was within that same lifetime that the larger Campbell family of Ohio lost contact with Mary Duncan Campbell and son Washington Campbell and his family as they moved to Illinois. Charles Campbell of Ironton, who was the keeper of family tree, notes that James W. Campbell died in Georgetown but he knew nothing of what happened to Mary, his wife, and had no record of the children of Washington. Washington was the termination of that line even though Washington's brother Hiram was living in Ironton to provide such information if Charles had asked. Eighty years later contact was made with a descendant of Hiram's who would not accept that Mary Duncan Campbell moved on with her son to Illinois. This modern cousin acknowledged there was no gravestone for in her in the Georgetown Cemetery but she must have been buried next to her husband.

By the same token, the grandchildren of Washington had no idea they had an uncle Hiram or cousin John that together were pioneers in the iron industry and founded Ironton. For that matter they did not know that Morton, Illinois, ninety miles up the road from the new homestead in Champaign, was founded by an uncle and cousins. As the grandchildren of Washington were growing up in Illinois, their cousins Elizabeth and Edith had become driving social forces in Cincinnati. If they read of the sisters in the newspapers it was with no connection.

Certainly such disconnection with family that moved on should come as no surprise. Disconnection was not the exception but most often the rule: out of sight, out of mind. Beyond this was the reality of war. Washington Campbell and family moved to Illinois a few years before the Civil War. When the war was over there was a national mindset to want to forget the past and move on. After the war the mood of the country was living in the moment with a romantic eye to the west and the future.

This was also a time of heightened immigration and with it people were holding less closely to ethnic circles. Marriages became a mix in a nation that was at least more and more a melting pot of European immigrants. It was also the time when the Campbells transferred their membership from the Presbyterian faith of their ancestors to the rural Methodist Church down the road—because it was convenient. It was a time of adopting names for children that were popular to the moment instead of the Scottish repetition of ancestor's forenames. Janet, Minnie, and Frank now appear with no reference to the past. The next generation has an Arlo, a tribute to a name in the family of the midwife who delivered the child.

Sometimes that loss of historical perspective is a personal prerogative. Some people simply do not like history. Stories of the past hold little reverence, as do family artifacts. The simple wooden box that contained the belongings of Rev. John Milton Campbell were shipped home from Africa to his mother Mary and she carried them with her out west to Illinois. The next generation, however, did not see the worth of holding on to such items. They took up space and except for the candlestick holder that was pretty, the rest was thrown away.

Ohio was now to become, at least for the grandchildren of Washington Campbell, a home forgotten as was Kentucky and the North River before that. To take their place would be a new home place, an Illinois home place, the last home place. Tradition, connection,and story would now be redefined by life on the Illinois plains; Illinois stories that would stretch in oral tradition to the end of the twentieth century.

In a sense, the moving to Illinois had parallels to the arrival of the Campbells in America. The past was left behind in the promise of the new. The wonder of the Campbell family in Ohio was now to sleep for a hundred years.

It was a home forgotten.

CHAPTER 13

THE LAST HOME PLACE

William Campbell   Elizabeth Wilson Campbell

James, *Charles, John W., Joseph N., Elizabeth, Mary, Rebecca, Samuel, Phoebe, Sarah, Fidelia*

Nancy, **Washington,** *Elizabeth, Hiram, Eliza, John Milton*

Greenleaf Washington, Agnes, James M., Caroline, Mary, John M., Ann Eliza

In the summer of 1854 the Illinois Central Railroad placed lands on the market on either side of its newly laid tracks. Carlton J. Corliss wrote, "The land office in Chicago was besieged by applicants eager to take advantage of the railroads' low prices and liberal credit terms under which some of the richest farmlands in Illinois could be purchased for a down payment of only 50 cents an acre, with seven years to pay the remainder."[1]

Such opportunity was ripe for the land speculators. One such land speculator was Richard Cloyde, a new immigrant from England who arrived in Champaign County in July of 1855. Richard quickly purchased the entire six hundred forty-acres of Section 34 of what would become Hensley Township. He then waited for the "pouring in" of farmers. Just weeks after he had purchased the land from the railroad, he met Washington Campbell.[2]

Washington and Eleanor Campbell, grandmother Mary Duncan Campbell, and her sister, Jane Duncan, had most likely traveled by steamboat from Ripley, Ohio, to Cairo, Illinois. Cairo is where the newly built Illinois Central railroad reached north to Chicago, stopping at the Doane House, which was the train station-hotel two miles west of Urbana at "West Urbana," soon to be the town of Champaign.[3]

203

On October 24, 1855, Washington Campbell purchased two lots in the town of Urbana. That same day he paid Richard Cloyde, $311.52 for one hundred twenty-acres of farmland in Hensley township, northwest of Champaign. This farmland would be in the family for five generations; one hundred forty-eight years. It would become the last home place.

As for Richard Cloyde, he gathered his earnings from Champaign real estate and made his way to Syracuse, New York. There Richard pursued his trade as an upholsterer, a very, very affluent upholsterer.[4]

Washington Greenleaf Campbell

Eleanor Jane Lilley Campbell

* * * * * * * * *

1855 was the exciting year of promise for the Campbells. 1856 was the year of despair. It takes real discernment to piece together the incongruities between the cemetery records, the DAR records, the 1850 census, and the tombstone record itself. The picture that finally emerges is one of profound grief.

Not even in her new home a year, Washington's wife,

The Last Home Place

Eleanor Jane Campbell died at the age of forty-four. In that same year Washington laid to rest his eldest daughter Elizabeth D. Campbell, who was twenty-four years old.[5] In this same year word came from Brown County, Ohio, that Mary's granddaughters, Eliza Evans and Jane K. Maklem, had died. They both were twenty years old. Then came the word of the death of aunt Phoebe Campbell Martin. Washington also bore the grief of fellow sojourner Robert Smith who came from Brown County, Ohio, to Champaign the same time as the Campbells. Robert lost his wife in March of 1856. Her name was Lucinda Rankin Smith, daughter of Rev. John Rankin.[6] The next year Washington's oldest sister Elizabeth Duncan lost her husband. Elizabeth left Brown County and moved to Champaign to be with her mother and brother.

Sometimes death comes in seasons, and this season must have been devastating to Washington. Within months of Eleanor Jane's and his daughter's death, Washington buys up the acreages on the south edge of Champaign that surround two sides of the cemetery that bears his wife's and daughter's remains. On March 30, 1857, Washington paid the premium of five thousand and forty dollars for this land, over fifteen times what he paid for the home place in Hensley township.[7] It must have been very important for Washington to uproot from the home and farm he had just established to purchase and move next to the land where his wife and daughter were buried. One year after buying the land near the cemetery, second daughter Eleanor W. Campbell died. It was 1858 and Eleanor W. was twenty years old.

By 1860 the Campbells were living on the new farm south of Champaign while still working the homestead in Hensley township. To work the land, Washington had himself and two sons of age. He also had three hired hands living on the south farm.[8] With his mother and now sister Elizabeth Evans to manage the house along with his older daughters, Washington was free to pursue his own interest in real estate. What happened to Richard Cloyde could happen to him. Within ten years of arriving in Champaign, Washington had purchased over twelve pieces of property, holding them until demand would create a desired profit.

It was a profit unrealized.

On September 17, 1868, Washington Campbell suddenly died of typhoid fever. The *Champaign Gazette and Union* published this notice:

> DIED:
> *In this city, on the 17th, of typhoid fever,*
> *Washington Campbell in the 63rd year*
> *of his age.*
> *Mr. Campbell was one of the oldest and most*
> *respected citizens and his loss will be mourned*
> *by all who knew him. He ever walked uprightly*
> *before God and man and has, ere this,*
> *received the reward of a faithful and virtuous*
> *life.*

The settling of Washington's estate was no small task. It was not just the farm to reconcile but the additional lands he held. The family also needed to settle with those from whom Washington had borrowed to make his investments. Land held in speculation that would someday bring a premium must now be sold as quickly as possible at below the market value.

To administer the estate would take three years, a long three years. It was a task left to Washington's middle son, John Milton Campbell, who was named for his uncle the missionary. It was in the pressure to at least break even with his father's estate that John Campbell opened an old wound.

The Last Home Place

On May 9, 1857, as Washington Campbell was just beginning in land development in Illinois, he assumed the mortgage for $1,350.00 in land belonging to Mr. A. Fink who lived in Scott County, Iowa, not far from the city of Davenport. It was a mortgage to be paid in full in two payments in 1858.[9] Why Washington was assuming the mortgage of someone one hundred fifty miles from Champaign is not known and would not have ever been known had not the following events unfolded and been recorded in his estate.

On the very same day that A. Fink mortgaged his land to Washington, he turned around and put the land in trust, borrowing an additional $1,177.00 against the same land and stating in the trust that if Mr. Fink didn't pay back money borrowed against the trust that the trust holder could sell the land. The trust agreement reached the courthouse two days before the mortgage with Washington was officially filed. Thus the trust had precedence. It was a legal requirement that the trust transaction be published in an area newspaper. Mr. Fink proceeded to publish the trust transaction in a small weekly newspaper at the far end of the county in Burlington, Iowa, with a circulation of only five hundred.[10]

By the time Washington found out that he had been taken for a ride by Mr. Fink, it was too late. It was a hard lesson in land investment. He had to take the loss, but it was a sore issue that lingered not only with Washington but now with his children as they were trying to settle his affairs.

Son John Campbell decided that he needed that $1,350.00 mortgage money to pay his father's debts. Thus, twelve years after the fact, John Campbell took the current owner of the Scott County land to court to get settlement against the mortgage. John lost; after all, twelve years was a long time. Still, John would not give up. He forced the issue to the Iowa Supreme Court on the grounds that A. Fink disclosed his financial maneuverings in an obscure newspaper that was published just once a week.

The Iowa Supreme Court in "Campbell vs. Tagge" understood the frustration, but, technically, Mr. A. Fink had played the law to his advantage without breaking it. Thus, on top of other financial obligations, John Campbell now had an additional lawyer and court fees to pay. On December 28, 1870, Attorney James T. Lane of Davenport, Iowa, wrote to John Campbell, " This of course settles the case against us as I am sorry to inform you of my cost which I very much regret, but what can't be helped must be born with patience."[11]

It was now down to selling the south farm, or at least a part of it. Nearly half of the Washington Campbell farm was on the west side of the road to the cemetery. John sold the west half of the farm at public auction.

Public notice of the sale of part of Washington Campbell's land

Today, that land that was sold in haste to pay Washington's debts is the football stadium of the University of Illinois. Fifty-six years after the Campbell acreage was sold, Red Grange the "Galloping Ghost" scored five touchdowns in one game against Michigan—five touchdowns running through what once was Washington Campbell's corn fields.[12]

The University of Illinois Marching Band at Memorial Stadium standing in formation in Washington's corn field.

* * * * * * * * *

Not only do the estate papers of Washington Campbell tell us of his losses to Mr. Fink, they also bear notice of a special sadness: a public announcement in the *Union Gazette* that Washington's twenty-one daughter Caroline L. Campbell was nowhere to be found either "concealed in the state or living beyond."[13] The notice was given in order to proceed with the sale of property. The notice also points out that Caroline was not aware of her father's death. She had lost touch with everyone. In fact, she had been gone for some time. She was was not even listed in the 1860 census when she was twelve years old. At some point in this mystery, Caroline had gone west, for we find reference to her in 1892 living in Hoquiam, Washington, with the married name of Caroline Greenhagen.[14]

There was a void when later in life the children of Washington Campbell gathered for a family photograph. A close look at the photograph reveals the insert of a picture of Caroline added to the family portrait so that the picture might be complete.

The Children of Washington and Eleanor Campbell

(Back Row l-r) Greenleaf Washington Campbell, Agnes Campbell Hannah, James M. Campbell

(Front Row l-r) Caroline Campbell (insert), Mary Campbell McCanaughy, John M. Campbell, Ann Eliza Campbell Gray

The Last Home Place

✶ ✶ ✶ ✶ ✶ ✶ ✶ ✶ ✶

Washington and Eleanor Campbell

Greenleaf Washington Campbell, Agnes Campbell Hannah, **James M. Campbell**, Caroline Campbell, Mary Campbell Mccanaughy, John M. Campbell, Ann Eliza Campbell Gray

Washington's mother, Mary Duncan Campbell, died in 1863, the same year her grandson, James M. Campbell, married Sarah O. Cook. This time of transition marked a shift of family focus from Washington's farm south of Champaign back to the original home in Hensley Township where Eleanor and daughter Elizabeth died.

James M. Campbell was twenty-eight years old when he married eighteen-year-old Sarah Cook in November of 1863. Eight months before they were married, James expanded the home place with a purchase of forty acres of land from the Illinois Central Railroad and then eventually added forty more acres to the north making a farm of two hundred acres.

The home place was prime farmland but only after much attention including the draining of swamp areas that were infested with poisonous snakes. If James and Sarah lived in the home built by Washington in 1855-56, it was only until a new home could be built. The old home was farther back from the road. The only reference we have to the original house was that it had a summer kitchen and it was in that kitchen that Washington continued his practice of harboring fleeing slaves heading north to Canada.[15]

Early maps of the region identify the Campbell home place in Hensley township as an area landmark, and eldest daughter Janet shared that the Campbell home was a center of activity in the township. Daughter Janet also mentioned that her mother Sarah was one of the first women in the area to have a sewing machine. It was manufactured by the White Sewing Machine Company and its novelty and efficiency gave reason for women of the area to gather to sew.[16] The Campbell farm had also kept an ice-storage shed where ice from frozen ponds was kept into the summer, saved for making homemade ice cream.[17] These were good times, a joy translated into thanksgiving as James M. Campbell led the singing in the Mount Vernon Methodist Church down the road.[18]

The very earliest memory of oldest daughter Janet was of a cake her mother had baked, probably commorating the day that Abraham Lincoln had died. Sarah responded by draping the sides of the cake in black crepe to mourn his passing.[19]

Marriage license for James M. and Sarah Cook Campbell

The Last Home Place

Wedding photographs of James and Sarah Campbell

Looking west toward the Campbell home

James and Sarah Campbell had five children that lived to adulthood. Janet, the eldest, was born September 14, 1864, followed by William on February 26, 1868. Minnie was born on November 17, 1875, Franklin on March 22, 1878, and then daughter Sarah on March 12, 1884. There may have been a sixth child that died in infancy as the birth registration of Franklin Campbell mentions him not as the fourth but the fifth child of James and Mary. No mention exists beyond this of another child.

James, Sarah and daughter Janet and son William, circa 1871

In the tax assessment of 1872 James M. Campbell records only ten head of cattle and seven hogs.[20] Such livestock would only speak to just beyond the immediate needs of the family and it would also indicate that the farming operation was grounded in the raising and selling of grain. In a history of Hensley township it was written that most early farmers in the township "used ox-teams in breaking the soil, generally four yokes to the plow. After the soil was turned, corn was planted, generally getting a moderate crop without further cultivation, also wheat succeed well on newly broken ground."[21]

The Last Home Place

The previous comment regarding the success in raising wheat rings a bell. Washington grew up in the spell of his father's interest in the production and selling of wheat fans mentioned in a previous chapter. It may well be that what grew best (wheat), the early money crop of Hensley Township, was what the Campbells knew best. And more, when the crop was harvested the season brought a let up in the schedule of the farm and provided the freedom for a new American experience—a vacation. For at least a break during the long winters the Campbells would travel by train to enjoy the warmth of Brownsville, Texas.[22] That is, until the year 1884. That April, Sarah, age forty, died just three weeks after child Sarah was born.

Sarah's death left James M. Campbell with a farming operation and five children to raise. Such circumstances as this happened with some frequency in these times and before. Complications in or from childbirth was a major cause of early death of women. When a husband was left to care for both family and farm, it was not unusual for him to send the children to extended family or even put them temporarily in orphanages and go and find another wife. Marriage was often a pragmatic arrangement. A father raising a family of five children alone bore the larger family's respect and concern.

James did not go looking for another wife. He held the family together with the help of his oldest daughter Janet. Janet was, at age twenty, the mother to her newborn sister Sarah (called Sadie), her six-year-old brother Frank, and nine-year-old sister Minnie.[23] Brother William was nearly of age and he too became central to keeping the family as one. Janet would not marry and have a home of her own until age thirty-four when all but sister Sadie were raised.

The earliest "casual" on-site family photos of the Campbells came four years after Sarah's death. It was the summer of 1888 and James' sister Agnes and family were visiting from Ohio.

Gathering at the Campbell farm's side porch

(Front Row) William Campbell, Sarah Campbell, Janet Campbell, Eura Campbell, Lutie Campbell

(Seated) James M. Campbell, Ann Eliza Campbell Gray, Mary Campbell McConaughy

(Back Row) L. Hannah, ?, Agnes Campbell Hannah, George Hannah

Making do did not come without strains. Getting by was everyone's concern for infant daughter Sadie. Getting by was caring for son Frank, who one day brought out the water jug to the field crews and lost the end of a finger in the farm machinery. James became nurse maid, administering a healthy dose of medicinal whiskey and then sewing the finger up and tending the infection. Frank would, as an adult, muse that the only time in his life that he was intoxicated was when he was six years old.[24]

Still, these were traumas that had practical solutions.

Years later the same son Frank, sixteen years old, ran away from home. He placed his lunch pail in the apple tree and caught the train for Davenport, Iowa. He worked for six months as an assistant to a harness maker in Bennett, Iowa, before responding to his father's pleas to come back home.[25]

If son Frank was a worry to be worked through, daughter Sadie's struggle to grow up became too much for James. Sadie was a free spirit, and James, seeking to find structure for her life, enrolled Sadie in a girls' school in Springfield.[26] This was not effective and the want of caring for Sadie was a concern for James to the end of his life.

James M. Campbell's brother John M. lived on the next farm west in Hensley township. In 1896 the son of James married the daughter of John. The marrying of cousins was common practice within families up to the twentieth century. In this case it brought together two side-by-side family farming operations and grown children William and Isabelle would be in charge.

In time this necessitated further change. It was decided that John, who now was a widower, would move next door from his house to the home place and brother James M. Campbell, who had lived on the home place for thirty-five years, would move with daughters Minnie and Sarah into Champaign.[27]

217

James M. Campbell lived to see his first two grandchildren born, Jesse and William Hartwell Campbell. James also was there for the wedding of daughter Janet who had faithfully raised her siblings and was ready for a family of her own.

In 1900, two years after Janet's marriage, daughter Minnie was married to Deskin Crouch and they would make a new home in Pilot Mound, Iowa. Brother Frank followed them to Iowa and became a harness maker in Lake City, twenty-five miles from his sister Minnie.

This left sister Janet to care once more for the family in its need. This time she would tend her aging and dying father. James M. Campbell died at Janet's home in 1901.

The occasion of their father's death brought all the children back to the home place. On the occasion of their father's funeral the five grown children posed for a family portrait.

The five children of James M. Campbell
(Left to Right) Frank, Janet, Sarah (Sadie), Minnie, William

The Last Home Place

Following the death of James, John and Janet Campbell Kenworthy moved to Iowa, first living with her sister Minnie and near her brother Frank. For a short time, half the family had relocated in close proximity in westcentral Iowa and for many years sister Minnie Campbell Crouch's home was a gathering place for the larger Campbell family.

This does not mean, however, that family did not come back to the home place in Champaign. In fact, the home place was a reason for a get-away. Frequently, family showed up in Champaign with no advanced notice.[28] They had come home. Some of the extended Campbell family would on occasion come to help on the home place with the harvest, and in 1918 a family reunion was held. All but one of James M. Campbell's children came to the reunion. Son Frank and his family were living at the far corner of North Dakota and could not attend.

The Family Reunion of 1918 on the Home Place

(Left to Right) Clara Campbell with one of her twins Francis, Clair is held by Olive Kenworthy, Janet Campbell Kenworthy, Sarah Campbell Cappock, William Campbell, John Kenworthy, William Hartwell Campbell, Mr. Cappock, (On Ground) Marvin Crouch, Roy Crouch, and John Kenworthy

Of particular note in this photo is that son William is standing near his son William Hartwell Campbell without wife Isabelle. Isabelle died of heart failure in 1914.

* * * * * * * * *

I was living near Marathon, Iowa, in 1978. Marathon was where my grandfather Frank ran a harness shop. On a visit to Marathon I was fortunate to meet an aged man who remembered my grandfather back in 1926. Not only did he remember Frank Campbell, but he remembered his work. If someone brought a harness in that needed repair, Frank not only repaired it but soaked it in linseed oil overnight making it look new. He took pride in doing more than what was asked and it is a tribute to him that after fifty years that workmanship was still remembered and honored. Still, as much as Frank did quality work, he was not a businessman. He did not have the business instincts nor the resolve to get payment for credit he extended to customers. Seldom did he get ahead, and once when he did, it was suddenly consumed in a needed surgery for his daughter. The struggles of Frank and Mollie Campbell are captured in the family biography *The Last Pioneers* written by the author.

In the summer of 1925 there was great excitement at the Frank and Mollie Campbell home. Frank's brother William was coming to visit. William had remarried and was the father of twin sons, Francis and Clair, and was living in Hollywood, California. To be sure William was also keeping the home place operation going back in Champaign but that was secondary now to his prime interest: real estate. William lived the spirit of his grandfather Washington, heading west and investing in land.

Sixty years later the children of Frank Campbell still talked of the time of Uncle Will's visit. My father told and retold of hearing his Uncle Will say to his brother Frank as they sat on the front porch, "The only way you will get ahead is to invest."

Frank responded, "I'm not a gambler."

The Last Home Place

To which Will said, "Every farmer is a gambler."[29] Certainly William Campbell had proven the possibilities. Investment risks in land in California in the 1920s were proving profitable. Not only had Will moved to Hollywood but bought the home that actor Harold Lloyd had built for his mother.

California was the good life at least until 1929. That was a hard year for the Campbells—all of the Campbells. In February Frank died of a heart attack in Landsford, North Dakota, age fifty. Sister Minnie came to the funeral and at the funeral there were flowers from "Hollywood Florist." Not knowing that Hollywood Florist was a national chain, the family assumed the flowers had come from Uncle Will. In fact, William had not even been told his brother had died until he received a thank you for the flowers he never sent. A year later Frank's wife Mollie loaded up her five children into an open-top Model-T Ford and made the five-hundred-mile trip on dirt and mud roads back to Iowa.[30]

That same year, the Great Depression brought falling real estate values. The investments of William and his partner plummeted. Life was a scramble to cover losses. In the end, William covered not only his own losses but the losses of his partner. He did so by mortgaging the home place. The farm was the saving grace of loss of fortune, and it was to the farm that William and wife Clara returned to weather out the depression.

William was not weathering out the storm of those years alone. Sister Minnie's husband, Deskin Crouch, was the owner of the Pilot Mound Bank that, like so many other small banks, went under. Uncle Deskin was remembered for the honor that in time he paid back everyone who lost money with the bank.

William lived on the home place until his death in 1938. His wife Clara remained on the farm even as the farm became now the home of yet another generation. William's twin son

Clair and new wife Eloise moved to the home place and took great pride in its renewal. They stripped the walls of layers of paper and gave a new face not only to the house but to the whole farming operation.[31]

*Newly married
Eloise and Clair Campbell*

It was during these years that Clair's twin brother Francis became a soldier and would die a soldier in the American offensive of taking Okinawa. It was also during this time that the last generation was born to the home place. Allan Clair Campbell, born October 17, 1942, spent his first ten years on the old Campbell farm. It is in Allan's memories that we glimpse what life there was like.[32]

The Last Home Place

Eloise and new son Allan Campbell

The home was a classic two-story wood frame house with a large porch on the front or east side facing the road and a small entry porch on the north side, facing the driveway and barn. The front yard was large, fenced, and contained approximately ten very large mature maple trees, which shed their leaves in the fall in profusion (great fun for a child to play in). Just north of the fence was the water well with the old wind-mill structure still standing.

The kitchen and summer kitchen were located on the west side of the house. The downstairs was made up of a large dining room off the main entrance, a living room with stairs to the upper floor, a master bedroom and my small bedroom adjacent. The single bathroom was located off the dining room with a shower on the back entry porch. Off the kitchen was the pantry with hooks to hang the hams. The plumbing, a modern innovation, was entirely located in the southwest corner of the home serving the bathroom, shower, and kitchen sink. Electrical wiring did extend throughout the home, but with the old-fashioned screw-in plugs for appliances. The telephone was located in the dining room—a party line—a long ring and two shorts for us, but there were other listeners from time to time.

Upstairs were two large bedrooms with tiny closets, a small bedroom on the west and a small storage room on the northwest with stairs to the living room. Our hired man lived upstairs in one of the bedrooms, but shared the bath with the rest of us.

The basement was small with a coal-burning furnace and a water softener composed of a complex of pipes that had to be mechanically recycled by my father after adding salt in a process that suggested operating a submarine. There were storage shelves for old jars of fruit and vegetables. Periodically, the "clinkers" or residual silicates from the coal had to be removed from the furnace, which looked to me as a child like Dante's Inferno. My father had to stoke the furnace regularly during the winter until he purchased the auger or self-feeder, using finely-ground coal which only needed to be refilled daily.

North of the house was the main barn, an ancient and honorable structure of hand-cut wooden beams held together by carved mortise and tenon with wooden pegs. Hand-forged iron nails and spikes were used elsewhere in the barn, which had previously included a blacksmith shop on the southeast corner. The large hayloft was great fun. East of the barn was the crib, holding the ears of corn on the sides and grain, such a soybeans and wheat, in the overhead bins. The corn had been previously picked by hand, loaded into horse-drawn wagons and driven to the crib for storage and natural drying. When sold, the sheller machine would arrive and the neighbors would gather to help with the process of removing the corn from the cobs and taking

The Last Home Place

it to the elevator, a few miles south at Rising. A great harvest dinner was a part of that annual ceremony. I also remember the numerous rats and mice that would end their feast and run around the crib at that time. A scale for weighing the wagons was located just to the south of the crib. Just north of the barn and crib was the hog house, a small open building, providing shelter from the sun and rain. Just north of the house and west of the barn was the garage for the cars and the buggy shed, used for storing farm equipment. Some old walnut trees were located just to the north of the buggy shed.

West of the house was the milk house and garden shed. Milk was carried to the milk house for separation of the cream and storage until the milk truck could pick it up for sale. The various buckets and equipment were washed in the milk house as well. Farther west was the large chicken house, smoke house, and dairy barn with a large water trough for the animals closer to the house. Just north of the chicken house was the pony pasture with a small shelter. South of the house had been a large garden and orchard, prior to my time. Large iron kettles were nearby for rendering fat when hogs were butchered. A long lane extended west between the field to the most westerly field on the farm. Northeast of the barn lot along the road was the tenant house, where the Drennan family lived. They had an older son Melvin and a younger daughter Anita, my neighborhood friends. That small house had no indoor plumbing, but only an outhouse and well, with water heated on the stove for the Saturday-night bath. Mr. Sam Drennan was a mechanic, working in town and Mrs Drennan kept a nice home for her family.

The northeast portion of the farm had always been pasture for the horses and cattle. A large cottonwood tree was in the center, which my father had removed with dynamite and a bulldozer when I was two or three years of age. I recall that he would not allow me to watch due to the danger of flying wood fragments, which did cover about a quarter-mile radius—

perhaps a bit too much dynamite. When the field was plowed for the first time, a pale ring of soil was noted. My father had someone from the University of Illinois come out to see it and they pronounced that it was an old Indian ceremonial fire ring. We never found many other artifacts, however.

My father grew corn, soybeans, wheat, and hay. Early on, he had a dairy herd and milked the cows morning and evening. He carried the milk in buckets to a clean room in the building just west of the house to separate the cream and keep it cool for pickup by the milk truck each day. At one time, he built numerous wooden hog houses and we raised Hampshire hogs. Later, he had a large herd of Hereford cattle. We also had lots of chickens and I would gather eggs.

Aerial view of the home place

Interesting experiences while growing up included seeing a large snake crawl out from under the summer kitchen steps on the northwest side of the house while I was pedaling my tricycle along the walk—a scary experience. I only saw one other snake on the farm, which my father caught by the tail as it exited the buggy shed, swung it around and snapped off the head. Prior to draining the property with tile, there were ponds, which were said to be home to copperhead and cottonmouth snakes—gone by my time, thank goodness. I enjoyed a swing in the front yard and a small tree house in the backyard when quite small. I also had a rabbit hutch in the backyard with many large white rabbits. We also had several dogs over the years. It always seemed cool in the big yard under the great maple trees, laid out similarly to the James W. Campbell farm north of Ripley, Ohio, in two rows in front of the house.

One spring, Dr. George Hunt, our veterinarian and good friend, came out to vaccinate the newborn pigs. I was probably four or five years old at the time and quite interested. Dr. Hunt used a syringe with a long needle and a shiny metal holder with three finger holes, so it could be operated with one hand. At the end of the series of vaccinations, as I was pressing in to see all, he reached over and took my arm, saying to my father, "I believe that we have just enough vaccine to do the boy!" At that point, my hair stood up on end and he let me slip away. I ran to the house and locked doors that had not been locked in decades!

When I was five years old, I received my pony Brownie. I had been persistently requesting a pony for some time and we visited the Kennedy Pony Farm near Taylorville that year. Soon thereafter, my father took the old war surplus truck there and returned with my pony. She was a gentle and patient pony, brown, of course, with a white mane and tail. We had a very nice saddle and bridle and I rode her virtually everyday for a year inside the yard, until I had to go to school. As I grew older, I rode her around the farm and even later around the neighborhood, sometimes on Sunday afternoon with Melvin Drennan, who had a horse. Later, she had three colts, Lightning, Star, and Squire, which we raised and trained.

Home Forgotten

Allan with his pony Brownie

There was a one-room school just one mile to the west of our home, Bunker Hill School, with just a few children. My father played Santa Claus at the school one year and I announced that Santa had my father's ring on!! Just before I was to enter first grade, the schools consolidated and I entered Dunham School, a mile east of our home, again a one-room school with an outhouse, but a bit larger. It had wonderful swings and a merry-go-round that would throw sparks if you got it going fast enough for the inner rail to rub on the center steel post at night. The hot lunch program was a single hot plate, used to heat your can of soup one day and your baked potato the next. Older students helped the younger students. Mrs. Knot kept order in the school and directed the eight rows of students, a total of twenty five or thirty.

By the third grade, the schools had further consolidated and a new brick school was opened for grades one through six in three rooms with a large community room and a kitchen for true hot lunches. To raise funds for the school, the parents put on several plays, one of which was a mock wedding (all men) with the largest farmer being the bride! It brought down the house and was a great success.

The Last Home Place

Growing up on the farm was a great adventure. Even when I was a baby, I loved the farm equipment. My mother often said that my father would have to park the tractor behind the shed when I was in my highchair, otherwise, I would be too excited to eat my lunch. When I was older, we built a larger tree house in a maple in the front yard, some twenty feet above the ground. That tree had a branch that extended from the trunk parallel to the ground for some five feet, making a natural place for the floor of the tree house. We had wooden boards as steps on the trunk of the tree, climbing up the side opposite the tree house and through a notch to the entrance.

We would pull things up by a rope to the tree house. Great fun. Later, we dug a cave, covered it with boards, canvas, and dirt with a little fireplace at the end for light. We used clay tile for the chimney. The barn lot was a giant playground for building dirt roads and other adventures.

As I grew older, I would do chores on the farm and learned to drive the tractor and truck at about twelve years old. I helped with baling the hay, a job that most people do not like. I remember one perfect day with the sweet smell of fresh hay, a good productive day, a steak and salad dinner and a beautiful sunset in the west. Each season on the farm has its own beauty and wonder, with anticipation for the next season.

In 1953 we moved up the road one mile to the north to land that had belonged to my mother's family. There my parents built a new brick home.

In 1968 my father died suddenly of a heart attack. The house on the home place had already been rented for some time and now a share-crop arrangement was made with the Hammel family to continue the farm operation.

As the Interstate highway system was developed through Champaign, a twelve-acre strip of the Campbell farm was accessed by the state to build Interstate 57. This left an eight-acre plot on the far side of the interstate that the family continued to farm until it was given as a gift to the University of Illinois. That gift, in honor of Clair and Eloise Campbell, supported the Mediterranean Gallery of the University's Spurlock Museum.

In 1999 the home place was sold and became the westward expansion of the city of Champaign. Where the last home place once stood is now the new Christie Medical Clinic. What is left of the old home place are photographs and memories.

The home place in winter's glory

CHAPTER 14

DISCOVERY

It was the summer of 1963. It was the summer of the long-awaited Campbell reunion and the only real family reunion I ever knew, at least Campbell family reunion. The grandchildren and great-grandchildren of James M. and Sarah O. Campbell were gathering at our home in the mountains of Colorado. The reunion was held at the Campbell home in Colorado because it was more central than Illinois to family coming from California, New Mexico and Oklahoma. All the children of James and Sarah Campbell were there except those of the home place, Clair and Eloise. Clair could not get away from farming operations.

To a youth of fifteen, all these people from so many places fit the general category of "relatives." At fifteen there was not a lot of connection to these elders of the family nor really a lot of interest in the stories they told of their parents. They were all strangers vaguely connected to the Campbell family but none of them bore the Campbell name. I had to listen well to understand the connection. I had never met a relative beyond my immediate family with my last name. That would come later.

For now there was this interest of my Aunt Gertrude Campbell Carver and cousin Olive Harris, daughter of Janet Campbell who raised her siblings so many years before. Olive was from Oklahoma. There was someone named Eloise Campbell in Illinois who lived near the home place and a wife of a cousin in Indiana. They were trying to put together a family history. We all were the scattered family of the home place in Illinois and before that somewhere near Ripley, Ohio, and before that Flemingsburg, Kentucky.

Home Forgotten

Grandchildren of James M. and Sarah O. Campbell gathering in Beulah, Colorado, summer 1963

(Standing) Chester Reynolds, son of Sarah; Robert Crouch, son of Minnie; Arlo Campbell, son of Frank

(Sitting) Julia Johnson, daughter of Janet; Olive Harris, daughter of Janet; Leota Knowlton, daughter of Frank; Gertrude Carver, daughter of Frank

* * * * * * * * *

In 1969 undergraduate school was over and graduate studies at the University of Illinois were about to begin. The chance to attend Illinois created a stir among the family. I was going on in my education in the shadows of the home place that none of my family had ever seen. Our one-thousand-mile journey from Colorado ended in Champaign on a hot humid summer's day. It was the day after arriving in Champaign that I met for the first time Eloise Campbell, the wife of Clair. I remember how unusual it was to meet someone by the name of Campbell who really was family. That afternoon I saw for the first time the home place. As we walked around I tried to imagine the tree where my grandfather Frank had put his lunch pail and run away to Iowa and the barn where he first learned the harness trade. This coming home to a place I had never been was the beginning of the wonder of who my grandfather was and how my life was an extension of the decisions he made. From then on there would be many times when I would look out from the thirteenth floor of Sherman Hall to the land of the home place in the distance. Little by little it came to me that what once happened there was a part of who I am.

As I became lost in my studies, I also became more and more a friend of Eloise Campbell. She would come and take me to church on Sunday morning and then we would have lunch and sometimes a drive in the country. She also took me to the Mount Hope Cemetery where now the issue of family went beyond my grandfather to his father and the father before that and the mother before that. This distant grandmother Mary Duncan Campbell was born in the 1700s, but who was she and who was this James W. Campbell that was her husband?

Eloise Campbell and James Campbell at the tombstone of Washington Campbell

As the school year extended into late autumn, Eloise asked me if I would like to take a weekend off and go with her to St. Louis to see her son Allan and his wife Marlene. What I remember of that trip was meeting a new-found cousin who shared my last name and was completing his residency at Barnes Hospital. It was a visit of fun as Allan treated me to a ride inside the St. Louis Gateway Arch. It was also the beginning of a friendship that through the years has mattered in family, vocation, the humor of the day, the passing of life's milestones, and deep mutual appreciation of history.

In 1971 I left the University of Illinois with a master's degree and six months later entered seminary to begin my divinity studies. One day on the floor of the seminary was a pile of tossed books deemed no longer of use to seminary. A lover of books, I mulled through the lot coming upon a coverless copy of the biography of John Milton Campbell. At that time I had only enough information to surmise that this book was about that distant uncle I had heard the family mention. I was right. In a heap of discarded books I had stumbled across a piece of my own past. Saving that book in 1972 was an initiation to family history that was to become an obsessive passion.

A few years later my grandmother died. After her death I longed to hear her voice once more. I should have recorded it. I should have asked her to tell one more time of her years with my grandfather Frank that I never knew. A short time later my Aunt Gertrude, who was so interested in history, died and once again I missed the chance to record her memories. Aunt Gertrude, however, not only loved history, she kept it. When she died there was a whole box of family letters, three hundred pages of family letters that chronicled the family's life from 1918 to 1932. Copies were made of these letters and with them the previously mentioned book, *The Last Pioneers,* began to take form.

Discovery

In 1977 I shared a pastorate at First United Methodist Church in Storm Lake, Iowa, and for three years was the pastor to the family of Donovan and Lois Crouch. Donovan was the grandson of Minnie Campbell Crouch. That connection all the more fueled an interest in the larger family that gathered at our home in 1963. It was a special blessing to be a pastor to my cousin and his family and even more the blessing when Don and Lois Crouch became Godparents to our children.

By the early 1980s I had convinced my father to write of his life. *The Story of My Life* gave him great satisfaction and real pleasure to others to read, especially his grandchildren. Six years after his death his granddaughter Erin set one of the chapters of his life to music.

The writing of his life came with much discussion with his older sister Leota as to exactly how things happened and when. Not always did they agree and sometimes that disagreement bore raised voices over the simplest experiences. Once there was an incident regarding my father and his sisters jumping on the bed. My father said it happened one way. His sister, my Aunt Loty as we called her, insisted the jumping on the bed bore a different result. They argued back and forth until in exasperation my father said to me, "Jim, you write it down the way you think it happened and that's the way it will be."

By the mid-1980s I was married and had a family of my own. I was surrounded by past and future pulling in both directions. My father's growing interest in claiming his past led us in a two-car family pilgrimage to the distant plains of North Dakota. There, in Landsford in 1982, my father and I found the unmarked grave of Frank Campbell and placed a simple monument to mark his final rest. It was there that the search for the richness of the past became a deeply spiritual experience that is hard to put into words but one that those who delve passionately into family history understand.

After the trip to North Dakota, a concerted effort began to find out just where our Campbells came from. Hiring the first of a total six historians from Brown County, Ohio, we began to get a handle on the William Campbell family. It was during this year, 1983, that conversation with my cousin Allan led to membership in the Clan Campbell Society and receiving its journal. One year later the findings of our early research were printed in the journal connecting the present back not only to Ohio and Kentucky, but the family's arrival in Virginia. To be sure, it was a very flawed outline that reached back nine generations, but at least the outline was there and with that, history escalated from passion to obsession. It was time to pilgrimage to the ancestral holy land.

One trip to Ohio followed another and the accumulation of materials was reaching a critical mass that birthed the first Campbell history called *The Book of Origins*. The book spanned six centuries of the family, building on what others had submitted on the internet. It was completely wrong. Still, *The Book of Origins* was a first effort and one that was to be completed before we left for mission work in Alaska. Who knew whether any further work on family history would be completed. The year of our move north to Alaska was 1990.

* * * * * * * * *

All the while my obsession with family history was unfolding and being shared with my cousin Allan, he was finding his own avocation in history that took him to other ends of the earth, all the way to the shores of Turkey and the wonder of underwater archeology.

Allan had graduated from Washington University School of Medicine in 1967 and, after six additional years of specialty training, began practice in Peoria in 1973 as a pathologist. He joined a group of pathologists serving multiple hospitals in the region, ultimately becoming president of the group, a laboratory

that the Campbells had lived across the United States, soil from two hundred sixty years of moving on. Allan and I blessed the moment and then scattered the earth at the front of our home in celebration of our roots and tribute to our shared ancestry.

* * * * * * * * *

*Allan Campbell and James Campbell
scattering the earth of our ancestors' homes at the Campbell home in Alaska*

In the last years of the twentieth century this work reached a point where more and more family members were saying, "get this published." My wife was concerned that if anything happened, what would she do with a bookcase full of Campbell family research? Besides, she said, you do have a life beyond family history. Get it done. She was not alone in this assessment and directive. It had become a family chorus. "Dad, all this is a jumble. The only place where all this makes sense is in your head. You are a walking book. Write it down."

No sooner did the research for this book come to an end than something new would come up. It never ended. In fact, new material poured in faster the closer the project came to an end. There was always something else. One of those "something elses" was Ironton, Ohio. It was the discovery that Washington Campbell had a brother who was an ironmaster and that his cousin not only was also an ironmaster but the founder of Ironton, Ohio. A visit was in order. We just might find something in Ironton.

We had no idea.

1999 was the Sesquicentennial of the town of Ironton and my contact with Rev. Hal Demus at the First Presbyterian Church in Ironton became an invitation to come and share in the celebration of the town founded by our Campbell ancestors. The invitation was further extended to my cousin Allan and his wife Marlene.

So it was that Allan, Marlene, and I had a grand road trip to Ohio. What fun it was to explore Brown County, the homestead of James W. and Mary Duncan Campbell, the cemetery that bore the resting place of William and Elizabeth Campbell, and the town of Ripley, the faintest memory handed on in our family's oral tradition.

Discovery

Allan and James Campbell at the grave of William and Elizabeth Campbell

Then it was on to Ironton. Not only were we given wonderful accommodations but a welcome we had never anticipated. We were greeted at the mayor's office and given a tour of the town that included the Campbell homes, Campbell street, the old Campbell School, and the Campbell grave sites; all this from people who were more than gracious that the Campbells had come to celebrate Ironton's special anniversary.

The next day Allan and I shared in the worship service in the church of our ancestors, a service that began with the playing of bagpipes and the satisfaction of seeing first-hand the light pouring through the rose windows in memory of our uncle the Rev. John Milton Campbell. When the service was over we were guests at a special luncheon where the mayor of Ironton proclaimed June 27, 1999, as "James and Allan Campbell Day in the City of Ironton, Ohio." We were given a copy of the official proclamation along with a key to the city.

Through it all I kept looking at my cousin in disbelief. Not only did we find a town that bore the memory of our family, we were welcomed home in grandest style. What fun and celebration that day was. The Monday morning edition of the *Ironton Tribune* bore the headlines CAMPBELLS COME HOME TO IRONTON.

It was a prophetic headline.

The front page of Ironton Tribune, June 28, 1999

Photo by permission of Ironton Tribune

Discovery

* * * * * * * * *

The approach of the twenty-first century forced the need to face reality. The city of Champaign was rapidly expanding to the west and the old home place, now empty, was no longer habitable. The Campbell farm was sold in 1999 and was now open to development.

Something else was happening too. The Campbell lands had always been close to the University of Illinois. Some of them were eventually incorporated into the campus, including the stadium. We remember again that when the twenty acres of the home place were used to make the interstate interchange, eight additional acres were given to the university. When Clair and Eloise were farming they delighted in regular sojourns to the university for dinner and conversation. Allan and Marlene met at the university and their children would attend the university. Now Allan came to serve on the board of the university's newly emerging Spurlock Museum on the east edge of the campus.

Pathology that unfolded into an interest in underwater archeology was now manifested in a commitment to nurturing historical and cultural appreciation. The time and substance that Allan and Marlene gave to the newly-emerging museum brought appreciation from the University of Illinois. One of the exhibit halls of the museum is now known as the "Campbell Gallery" in honor of Allan, Marlene, and their children. The dedication of the Campbell Gallery included the words, "The Campbell Family name is one that lives on in the Spurlock Museum."[34]

The Spurlock Museum is not a passive exhibit of the past. It is a vital center of new perspectives on culture and its origins. It is a place to wonder as much of the future as to appreciate the past. To that end, the University Museum holds the Allan C. Campbell Family Lecture Series of distinguished scholars including underwater archeologist Dr. George Bass, Dr. Ian

Allan and Marlene Campbell cutting the ribbon of the Campbell Gallery at the Spurlock Museum of the University of Illinois

The Campbell Gallery, a room for special exhibits

Discovery

Jenkins of the British Museum, and Dr. Patrick McGovern of the University of Pennsylvania.

Outside are the walkways that lead to the central campus and beyond to the lecture halls of the university's south side. It is just a short walk from the museum and the Campbell Gallery to the graves of all those who came before, those whose names bear witness of two hundred seventy years of one family's seeking, finding, and moving on. It is fitting that as time and use change the character of the land, that those who worked its possibilities not only are remembered for what once was, but for the vision, the risk, and those values still echoing in their children. What a tribute to remember the past in new and wonderful ways that the Spurlock Museum affords not far from where the ancestors are laid to rest.

On the day in July when I visited the museum and bore appreciation and pride for my cousin's commitment to history, I walked the Campbell Gallery sensitive to its latest exhibition of African indigenous art. As I pondered the beauty of each piece, I found myself wondering what great-great-grandfather Washington would think. What would he say to see such a profound display of beauty open and offered to all from those whose distant cousins once ran frightened to his home in search of freedom?

Later, back home in Alaska, I received a copy of Dr. John Stone's book of poetry *Music From Apartment 8*. John Stone was the latest guest scholar in the Allan C. Campbell guest lecture series at the university museum. It was a cold wintry day in Alaska, a day for reading good poetry and this was good poetry, exceptional poetry, poetry that by week's end became a part of me and the focus of my Sunday's sermon. I relished the truth of the book even as I savored the thought that it came to me as an echo from what still remains of "the home place," the museum "where the family name lives on."

Home Forgotten

✻ ✻ ✻ ✻ ✻ ✻ ✻ ✻ ✻

To Our Children

The farms are gone now. Like most of the Campbells of Brown County, the Campbells of Champaign County have scattered to the wind. In a world going faster and faster, it is hard to imagine any future linkage of generations bound by any new home places. We are in such a hurry, afraid of being left behind by the world on the run. Then again, it is just such a world that might, just might, stir all the more a longing for connection—connection to a past that has something to give the moment and perhaps the future. It may be the oddest irony that from a disposable world with little memory, there may come a time of deep longing for memory, to seek and own and be blessed by the past once again. If so, then let this book serve as a road map to places and persons who once were and had something to say with their lives. Savor the sacredness of finding and walking their land. Seek the folder that holds William Campbell's spiritual journal of 1786—and just hold it. Run your hand across the names on the tombstones—your name—part of you that now has been lifted from the fog of forgotten.

We are still the Campbells of the North River—seeking, finding, moving on. Perhaps from such a past may come a thoughtfulness not only to make something of our lives but to leave something meaningful behind; something or some place or some memory for those who follow to wonder at what beauty there is in the world and in that wonder to feel the question—What would our grandparents and their parents and their parents before think of this? To reach for and live and hold and be held by that question is to discover the home place of the heart.

*Allan and James Campbell on the porch
of the last home place*

END NOTES

Chapter One

1. Charles Campbell, essay in *Historical Sketches of the Campbells, Pilchers and Kindred Families et al.*, by Margaret Campbell Pilcher, (Nashville: Press of Marshall and Bruce Co., 1911), 197.

2. Charles Campbell, correspondence to Lettie Green, September 24, 1907.

3. William Mitchell, "On the Trail of a Genealogy Mystery: The Duncan and Mary McCoy Campbell Lineage," in *Journal of the Clan Campbell Society,* 10 (United States of America), (Spring 1983), 20.

4. Charles Campbell, essay in *Historical Sketches,* 193 ff.

5. Charles Campbell, June 26, 1740, *Hisorical Sketches*, 199.

6. James Marcellus Campbell, quoted by Charles Campbell, *Historical Sketches*, 204.

7. Charles Campbell, essay in *Historical Sketches,* 194.

8. Merrill D. Anthoby, ed., *A Memorial and Biographical Record of Iowa,* vol. I. (Chicago: The Louis Publishing Company, 1896), 175.

Chapter Two

1. Katherine Bushman, correspondence to author, March 7, 1984. "The records enclosed will show to you that placement of Charles Campbell in the Pilcher book is incorrect. Charles Campbell and brother Hugh lived in the area today that borders on Rockingham County, along the North River of the Shenandoah. The distance to the North River of the County is more like 15 miles. Their lands were actually between present day route 42 and Centerville—which is east of route 42."

2. Charles Campbell, essay in *Historical Sketches*, 204.

3. William and Robert Brown, deed to Robert Campbell, May 20, 1752. Augusta County Deed Book, no. 4, 201.

4. Administration of Estate of Robert Campbell deceased, August 19, 1768, Augusta County Records.

5. Two intense searches of available records by historian John McCabe in Belfast showed no indication of Robert, Charles, or Hugh Campbell in County Derry from 1700 to 1740.

6. Carole Gilmour, correspondence to author, March 15, 2006.

7. C.E. May, *Life Under Four Flags in North River Basin of Virginia* (Verona, Virginia: McClure Printing Company, 1976), 66.

8. Thomas Lewis, survey book 1745, survey no. 55. for Charles Campbell, June 15, 1745.

9. Estate Appraisement, Robert Campbell, November 15, 1768, Augusta County Records.

10. Ibid.

11. La Rachefoucauld-Liancourt, "Travels," quoted by Robert D. Mitchell in *Commercialism and Frontier: Perspectives in the Early Shenandoah Valley* (Charlottesville: University Press of Virginia, 1977), 130.

12. Thomas Lewis, survey, Charles Campbell, June 15, 1745.

13. C. E. May, *My Augusta*, (Bridgewater, Virginia: Good Printers, Inc., 1987), 1.

CHAPTER THREE

1. Katherine Bushman found it difficult to imagine that Robert's very aged wife Margaret would have been a co-executor of her husband's estate along with her sons in 1768. One option to this is that Margaret was the single daughter

of Robert. There is a line that claims that connection. Then again, Margaret may have been a second and younger wife.

2. Sale of 220 acres from Robert and William Brown to Robert Campbell, May 20, 1752, Augusta County Deed Book no 4, 201.

3. Though some Magill sources state that Esther Magill was already living in the American colonies, arriving with her family in the 1720s, a more likely scenario is that Esther came with husband Hugh in 1740 when he proved his importation and listed Esther and Sarah as co-travelers. All of the children of Hugh and Esther were baptized by Rev. Craig in the 1740s and '50s. Only first daughter Sarah is left from the baptismal roles. She was most likely baptized in County Down before the voyage to the colonies.

4. Lyman Chalkey, *Chronicles of the Scotch-Irish Settlement in Virginia,* vol I, Court Order Book II, February 16, 1748, 77.

5. The Families from the North River from County Down from Downpatrick to Dromore include the Andersons, Magills, Trotters, Campbells, and Fowlers.

6. Lyman Chalkey, *Chronicles,* February 15, 1748, 72.

7. Appraisement of estate of Charles Campbell, May 18, 1779, Augusta County Records.

8. Charles Campbell, essay in *Historical Sketches,* 210.

9. C.E. May, *Life Under Four Flags,* 25.

10. William Campbell, personal spiritual journal, Cincinnati Historical Society.

11. C. E. May, *Life Under Four Flags,* 113. William Bishop, servant, takes Charles Campbell to court for not paying William his freedom dues, August 22, 1755.

12. C.E. May, *Life Under Four Flags,* 97-98.

13. Charles Campbell, *History of the Colony and Ancient Domain of Virginia,* (Philadelphia: Lippincott and Company,

1860), 430.

14. Robert D. Mitchell, *Commercialism and Frontier: Perspectives in Early Shenandoah Valley*, (Charlotttesville: Univesity Press of Virginia, 1977) 1-14, 53

15. Charles Curry, correspondence, 1907 in "The Hunters of Naked Creek," website by Tracy Hunter, hhttp:/member.aol.com/th3978/index.html

16. Charles Campbell, essay in *Historical Sketches*, 205.

17. Washington and Lee University, historical paper no. 2, 85. quoted by Charles Campbell, essay in *Historical Sketches,* 197.

18. Charles Campbell indicates that most likely Mary and Charles Campbell's daughter Sarah married a Trotter cousin. Other sources suggest this Sarah Campbell Trotter is later mentioned in land transactions in Tennessee. The Trotters who settled on the North River were the family of James Trotter. This would make Mary Trotter Campbell and James Trotter brother and sister. It is brother James Trotter that establishes the link of the Trotters of Augusta County, Virginia with the Trotter family of Downpatrick, County Down.

CHAPTER 4

1. Imogen Benson Emery, *Genealogy of the Campbells, The Kerrs, The Wilsons, The Willsons, The Kirkpatricks, and their descendants in the United States*, (Mount Vernon, Iowa, 1960.)

2. Don McNeil, correspondence to author, July 30, 1986. "Imogene Emery not only made a leap of faith trying to establish Eilliam Campbell and Elizabeth Wilson as parents of James Campbell and Elizabeth Kerr, but she apparently tied Elizabeth Kerr to the wrong Kerr lineage."

3. Red Oak Presbyterian Graveyard. http:/wwwgeocities.com/jollygames/redoak.html

4. Wilson Family Genealogy, compiler unknown, Washington and Lee University Library.

5. Charles Campbell, *Historical Sketches*, 210.

6. David H. Fisher and James C. Kelly, *Bound Away, Virginia and the Western Movement,* (Charlottesville: University of Virginia Press, 2000), 136-137.

7. Craig Thompson Friend, *Along the Maysville Road*, (Knoxville, University of Tennessee Press, 2000), 64.

8. Ibid., 28-32.

9. Ibid., 16-20.

10. Ibid., 23-28.

11. "A sketch of the Life of the Late Judge Campbell," in *Biographical Sketches With Other Literary Remains of the Late John W. Campbell*, (Columbus, Ohio, Scott and Gallagher, 1838), 2-3.

12. Hiram Campbell, interview by W. H. Siebert. September 30, 1894, Siebert Collection, Ohio State Historical Society.

13. John W. Campbell, *Biographical Sketches* "To A Friend," 167-168.

14. John Milton Campbell, correspondence to Hiram Campbell, November 28, 1843, Miami University of Ohio Archives.

Chapter 5

1. Judge W. W. Gilliland, "A Brief Outline of the History of Red Oak Church Prior to 1835," *Ripley Bee*, September, 1898.

2. Records of the White Oak Presbyterian Church, *Draper Papers*, Wisconsin Historical Society. (16CC60-61)

3. *Georgetown Castigator*, October 23, 1832, 2.

4. "A Friend," reflections on the life of Joseph N. Campbell in *Biographical Sketches*, 275.

Chapter 6

1. *Biographical Sketches*, 2.

2. Nelson W. Evans and Emmus B. Stiner, *A History of Adams County, Ohio*, (E.B. Stiner, 1900), 301.

3. Allan Trimble, "Autobiography of Allen Trimble," in the *"Old Northwest" Genealogical Quarterly* 10, (1907), 45.

4. *Dictionary of American Biography,* vol III, ed. by Allen Johnson (New York: Charles Scribner's Sons, 1929), 460.

5. *Biographical Cylcopaedia and Portrait Gallery,* vol. II, (Cincinnati, Ohio, 1884), 447.

6. *Biographical Sketches*, 6.

7. Ibid.

8. John Campbell, correspondence to Allen Trimble, Washington City, April 2, 1824, printed in "Papers of Governor Allen Trimble," *Old Northwest Genealogical Quarterly 9* (October, 1906), 314.

9. *Biographical Sketches*, 6.

10. John Campbell, correspondence to Allen Trimble, Washington City, April 10, 1826, printed in "Papers of Governor Allen Trimble," *Old Northwest Genealogical Quarterly 9* (October, 1906), 314.

11. *Biographical Sketches*, p.155.

12. John W. Campbell, correspondence "To a Friend," Washington, January 17, 1823, Ohio Historical Society.

13. Allen Trimble, "Autobiography," in the *Old Northwest Genealogical Quarterly* 9, (October, 1906), 120. The autobiography mistakenly calls John "Samuel" in the narrative.

14. *Biographical Sketches*, 8.

15. *Biographical Sketches*, 11-12.

CHAPTER 7

1. A. Charles Campbell, essay in *Historical Sketches*, 211.
   B. Merrill D. Anthoby, ed., *A Memorial and Biographical Record*, 175.

2. Merrill D. Anthoby, ed., *A Memorial and Biographical Record*, 175.

3. Donald and Ruth Roth, *Morton: A Pictorial History*, (Morton, Illinois, 1977.), n.p. James Marcellus Campbell's, diary is quoted. The importance of the account of James' loss of a leg is underwritten by the fact that it was even mentioned in his obituary.

4. Allan Campbell, correspondence to author, August 2006.

5. Donald and Ruth Roth, *Morton*, n.p.

6. Ibid.

7. Merrill D. Anthoby, ed., *A Memorial and Biographical Record*, 176.

8. Donald and Ruth Roth, *Morton*, n.p

9. Atlas Map of Tazewell County, Illinois (Davenport: Iowa, Andreas, Lyter and Company), 145.

10. Roth, *Morton, A Pictorial History*, n.p.

11. Ibid.

12. Sharon Kouns, "John Campbell," in *Ironmaster Days, June 2-28, 1998, Ironton, Ohio*, 4. The Kouns essay, as other Ironton essays that recount this event, does not mention that William Humphreys was his uncle.

13. Eliese Bambach Stivers, *Ripley, Ohio: Its History, and Families*, (Ripley, Ohio: Eleise Bambach Stivers, 1965), 14.

14. *Biographical Encyclopedia of Ohio of the Nineteenth Century*, (Cincinnati and Philadelphia: Galaxy Publishing Company, 1876), 377.

15. *The Morning Irontonian*, November, 1907.

16. William W. Hearne, *The Iron Trade Review* 77 (October 22, 1925), 1023.

17. "Lucy Selina's Coke Era," in *Virginia Cavalcade*, (Autumn, 1957), 40.

18. Charles A. Waltman, "Influence of the Lehigh Canal on the Industrial and Urban Development of the Lehigh Valley" in "Proceedings of the Canal History and Technology Symposium." vol. 2., March 6, 1983, 94.

19. The involvement of Joseph G. Firmstone and his son William in the Hanging Rock Iron industry is told in the series of land transfers and legal disputes recorded in the following Lawrence County Court Records. Deed to Joseph Firmstone from John F. Gould, December 13, 1837. Mortgage deed for the same property, December 16, 1837. Deed John F. Gould to Joseph Firmstone, July 8, 1839. Nathaniel Hurd to Joseph Firmstone, November 16, 1837. Foreclosure of Firmstone operations by John F. Gould, July 10, 1845. Foreclosure by John F. Gould on Joseph Firmstone, May, 2, 1848. William Firmstone covering of debt of his father and selling the La Grange Furnace to john Campbell, September 14, 1850.

20. Craig L. Bartholomew and Lance E. Metz, "The Anthracite Iron Industry of the Lehigh Valley," (Center for Canal History and Technology, 1988), 16-17.

21. A. George T. Fleming, "A History of Pittsburg and Enviorns," *American Historical Society,* vol. III, (1922), 495.

 B. Will Price, Part 2 on Longdale, "Desponding Then Salvation," in *Allegheny Highlander*, September 1, 1982.

22. Eugene B. Willard, *A Standard History of The Hanging Rock Iron Region of Ohio,* vol. I, (Lewis Publishing Company, 1916), 270.

23. *Irontonian* Semi-weekly, November 15, 1907.

24. David T. Woodrow, correspondence to John Campbell, November 25, 1848. Archives, Lawrence County Historical Society Archives.

25. John Campbell, speech notes, 1846, Hanging Rock, Ohio. Lawrence County Historical Society Archives. See Eugene B. Willard's *The Standard History of the Hanging Rock,* 273.

26. The tensions between Robert Hamilton and John Campbell are best summarized by Phillip G. Payne, *Modernity Lost: Ironton, Ohio, In Industrial and Post-Industrial America*, unpublished volume. (St. Bonaventure, University, St. Bonaventure, New York, n.d.), 16-19.

27. The inception of what became Ironton bears mythic status as the story is told and retold of the Holloween Ride of John Willard and John Peters to awaken John Campbell with their support of his vision of a new town. See Eugene B. Willard's *The Standard History of the Hanging Rock,* 275.

28. Eugene B. Willard, *The Standard History of the Hanging Rock,* 275.

29. Sharon Kouns, "John Campbell," *Ironmaster Days,* 4-5.

30. *Ironton Register*, September 3, 1891.

31. John Campbell, correspondence to Hiram Campbell, April 30, 1849.

32. Marrion Blair Edmundson, correspondence to author, June 1, 1984.

33. *Ironton Register,* November 8, 1877

34. Elizabeth was the seventh child of William and Elizabeth Campbell to live to adulthood. Elizabeth married William Humphreys who was key to the early employment of nephew John Campbell. Elizabeth and William Humphreys' third child was John Wilson Humphreys. John Wilson Humphreys married Isabelle Rankin, the daughter of Rev. John Rankin. Their daughter Elizabeth married Colonel George N. Gray. Elizabeth Gray was a second cousin of John Campbell.

35. U.S. Census, 1860, Lawrence County, Lawrence County, Olive Furnace, Sarah Bimpson.

36. The Ironton-Lawrence County Community Action

Organization, "The John Campbell Story," (September 27, 1975), 4.

37. See Sharon Kouns' extensive review and periodical excerpts of the Ironton Campbell families and their descendants. Lawrence County Historical Society, Ironton, Ohio.

37. *Ironton Register*, September 3, 1891, 1.

38. *Oskaloosa Daily Herald*, June 17, 1805, 2.

39. Semira A. Phillips, ed., *Proud Mahaska: 1843-1900*, (Oskaloosa, Iowa: Harold Print, 1900), 713.

40. Merrill D. Anthoby, ed., *A Memorial and Biographical Record*, 176.

CHAPTER 8

1. Barry Horstman, *100 Who Made a Difference*, (Cincinnati: *Cincinnati Post*, 1999), 100.

2. Barry Hostman, "Edith Campbell: Activist Had A Passion For Justice," *Cincinnati Post*, September 24, 1999.

3. *Ladies Home Journal*, June, 1915, 32.

4. *Journal of Social Hygiene* 28.(March, 1942), 151.

5. Geoffrey S. Giglierano and Deborah A. Overmyer, *The Bicentennial Guide to Greater Cincinnati: A Portrait of Two Hundred years*, (Cincinnati: Cincinnati Historical Society, 1988), 447.

6. *Biographical Sketches*, 279.

7. *Biographical Sketches*, 275.

8. *Biographical Sketches*, 278.

9. Ibid.

10. Marguerite Zapolean, "Cincinnati Citizens: Elizabeth Campbell (1862-1945) and M. Edith Campbell (1875-1962)" in *Queen City Heritage*, 43 (Winter, 1985), 3-4.

11. Frances Hollingshead, "Ohio Women In Medicine – A Biographical Note," in *The Ohio State Medical Journal* 41:5, 829.

12. Barry M. Horstman, "Edith Campbell: Activist Had A Passion For Justice."

13. Betty Van Meter Ames, "Portrait of a Distinguished Alumna," 1962, in *Cincinnati Historical Society Collection*.

14. Marguerite Zapolean, "Cincinnati Citizens," 10.

15. *Ladies Home Journal,* June, 1915, 32.

16. Betty B. Ames, "Cincinnati's First Woman Citizen," in *Historical and Philosophical Society Bulletin* 2 (April 1963), 133.

17. The Academy of Political Science, *The Proceedings of the Academy of Political Science In The City of New York*, (New York, Columbia University, 1910), 151.

18. Betty Van Meter Ames, "Leading Woman Citizen of Cincinnati Dies," in *News of The Delta Kappa Gamma Society International* 20, (March, 1963), 2.

19. Barry M. Horstman, "Edith Campbell: Activist Had A Passion For Justice."

20. *Cincinnati Times-Star*, January 1, 1912, 12.

21. John M. Brewer, *History of Vocational Guidance Origins and Early Development*, (New York: Harper and Brothers, 1942), 92.

22. *Cincinnati Tribune*, "Finds Children Work Illegally," Septermber 13, 1915, 10.

23. *Ladies Home Journal*, June, 1915.

24. *New York Times*, "To Support World Court," September, 20, 1925, 18 and "Women Voters Hear Appeal For Peace," April 26, 1932, 2.

25. Betty Van Meter, "Portrait of a Distinguished Alumna,"20, Miami University of Ohio Archives.

26. *Cincinnati Times-Star*, "Woman Recipient of Unique

Honor, Doctor of Humanities, Pioneer in Work Among Children," June 13, 1931, 3.

27. Justice Felix Frankfurter, correspondence to Lockwood Thompson, January 30, 1940.

28. Elizabeth Campbell, *The Woman's City Club Bulletin* 2 (July 1917), 15-16.

29. Marguerite Zapolean, "Cincinnati Citizens," 8.

30. Cecil Striker, ed., *Medical Portraits* (Cincinnati: Academy of Medicine, Cincinnati, 1963), 53.

31. Frances Hollingswood, "Ohio Women in Medicine-A Biographical Note," p. 830.

32. Marguerite Zapolean, "Cincinnati Citizens," p. 4.

33. Cecil Striker, ed., *Medical Portraits*.

34. Marguerite Zapolean, "Cincinnati Citizens," 10.

35. Dedication Exercises, M. Edith Campbell Junior High School, May 25, 1969, 2.

36. Marguerite Zapolean, "Cincinnati Citizens," 3.

Chapter 9

1. R. W. Wilson, *The True Missionary Spirit, As Exemplified in the Life and Triumphant Death of John Milton Campbell, Late Missionary to Africa*, (Cincinnati: George L. Weed, 1847), 6.

2. Mason County Marriages, January 7, 1801.

3. James McConnell, *Biography of Greer Brown Duncan*, 1853.

4. Allan W. Eckhart, *The Frontiersman*, (Ashland, Kentucky: Jesse Stuart Foundation, 2001), 40.

5. Jane Duncan Stewart, April 29, 1842, appoints Washington Campbell her attorney to sell interest in estate of her dead father. Mason County Records.

6. John Milton Campbell, correspondence to Hiram Campbell, March 4, 1837 and February 1, 1839.

7. *Georgetown Castigator*, May 15, 1833, 6.

8. *Georgetown Castigator*, May, 1845.

9. W.H. Beers, *History of Brown County*, (Chicago: W. H. Beers and Company, 1883), 402.

10. R.W. Wilson, *The True Missionary Spirit*, 6.

11. John W. Campbell, correspondence to James W. Lilley, November 11, 1827.

12. R.W. Wilson, *The True Missionary Spirit*, 9.

13. John Milton Campbell correspondence to Hiram Campbell, September 1, 1836, Miami University of Ohio Archives.

14. John Milton Campbell, correspondence to Hiram Campbell, March 4, 1837, Miami University of Ohio Archives.

15. Ibid.

16. John Campbell correspondence to Hiram Campbell, April 30, 1849.

17. Research based on U.S. Census, Brown County, Ohio, 1850. William P. Maklem, p. 59. Duncan, Evans, p. 300. Georgetown tombstone of Eliza Jane Evans. Reaseach Pat Donaldson, genealogist.

18. Roster of members of the Ohio 89th Infantry who died at Andersonville Prison.

19. John Milton Campbell correspondence to Hiram Campbell, January 31, 1841.

20. Rutherford B. Hayes, correspondence to his wife, August 1, 1875. From Collected Letters of Rutherford B. Hayes, vol. III, chapter 31, 65-66.

21. L. T. Dean, diary, transcribed by Virginia Bryant.

22. *Ironton Weekly Register*, August 8, 1896.

23. *The Missionary Herald*, vol. xl (Boston: November, 1844), 380.

24. R.W. Wilson, *The True Missionary Spirit*, 1.

25. Ibid., 83.

26. Ibid., 5-6.

27. R.W. Wilson, *The True Missionary Spirit*, 8.

28. Ibid., 12.

29. Ibid., 15.

30. R.W. Wilson, The True Missionary Spirit, 48.

31. Ibid., 60.

32. Ibid., 52.

33. *The Tri-Weekly Cincinnati Gazette*, June 17, 1843, 1.

34. Th*e Tri-Weekly Cincinnati Gazette*, June 20, 1847, 1.

35. *The Watchman of the Valley*, November 16, 1843, 1.

36. R.W. Wilson, *The True Missionary Spirit*, 63.

37. *The Missionary Herald, vol. xl*, (Boston, November, 1844), 380.

38. R.W. Wilson, *The True Missionary Spirit*, p.66.

39. Ibid., 68.

40. Ibid., 65.

41. John Milton Campbell, correspondence to supporters of his work, January 1, 1844, New York.

42. R.W. Wilson, *The True Missionary Spirit*, 74

43. Ibid., 17.

44. Ibid., 75.

45. Albert Bushnell, *Missionary Herald, vol. xl* (Boston: November, 1844), 380.

46. Jeremy Rich, "A Workman is Worthy of His Meat: Labor Disputes, Food and Identity in Colonial Libreville 1860-1900," Southeastern Regional Seminar in African Studies, (Highland

Heights, Kentucky), 9-10.

47. Clifton Jackson Phillips, *Protestant America and the Pagan World: The First Half Century of the American Board of Commissioners For Foreign Missions, 1810-1860,*(Cambridge: Harvard University Press, 1969), 230.

48. Jeremy Rich, "A Workman is Worthy of His Meat," 6.

49. Robert Lilley correspondence to James Lilley, Lilley, Ohio, September 7, 1831.

50. Albert Bushnell, *Missionary Herald, vol. xli,* (May,1845), 158.

51. U.S. Census, 1850, Washington County, Byrd Township, Ohio, Washington Campbell.

CHAPTER 10

1. *Biographical Sketches*, 278.

2. "Underground Railroad," video produced by Triage. Inc. for The History Channel, 1999.

3. Paul R. Grim, " The Rev. John Rankin, Early Abolitionist," from master of arts thesis, Ohio State University, 1935, published in *Ohio Archeological and Historical Quarterly* , vol. 46, 227.

4. John Rankin, *Life of Rev. John Rankin, written By Himself In His 80th Year, 1872,* (reprinted by The Rankin House, September, 2004), 31-37.

5. Fergus M. Bordewich, *Bound For Canaan: The Underground Railroad and the War For The Soul Of America*, (New York: Armistad, Harper and Collins, 2005), 192-195.

6. Hiram Campbell, interview by W. H. Siebert, September 30, 1894.

7. W.W. Gilliland, "A Brief Outline of the History of Red Oak Church Prior to 1835."

8. J.J. Fueser, Anthony Dugdale, J. Celso de Castros Alves, "Slavery and Abolition," published by the Amistad

Committee, Yale University, 2001.

9. Obituary essay from "A Friend," in *Biographical Sketches*, 273.

10. *Biographical Sketches*, 172.

11. Robert Lilley, correspondence to James Lilley, September, 1831, Library of Virginia.

12. Gabriel Lilley, correspondence to William Lilley, Warren Kentucky, May 10, 1830, Library of Virginia.

13. William Lilley, correspondence to Jane Lilley, Lilly, Ohio, June 20, 1832, Library of Virginia.

14. Ripley Anti-slavery Constitution and Roster, Washington Campbell was member #185.

15. *The Cincinnati Observer*, "Lane Theological Abolition." January 14, 1841, 1.

16. John Milton Campbell, correspondence to Hiram Campbell, March 4, 1837, Miami University of Ohio Archives.

17. Hiram Campbell, interview by W. H. Siebert, September 30, 1894.

18. Hiram Campbell, interview by W. H. Siebert, September 30, 1894.

19. Paul Grim, "The Rev. John Rankin, 238.

20. U. S. Census, 1850, Brown County, Byrd Township, Washington Campbell.

21. Ann Hagedorn, *Beyond The River*, (New York: Simon and Schuster, 2002), 210.

22. Edith and Elizabeth Campbell dwelled often on the legacy of the Leavitt family of their mother's heritage. The Leavitt home was near to the Rankin home and eventually became a part of the Rankin farm. The Campbell sisters maintained that their grandfather, D.K. Leavitt, was one of the first three to join John Rankin in providing refuge for fleeing slaves.

23. R. Wilson, *The True Missionary Spirit*, 55-56.

24. John G. Fee, *Autobiography of John G. Fee* (Chicago: National Christian Association, 1891), 13-15.

25. Victor B. Howard, *The Evangelical War Against Slavery and Caste,* (Selinsgrove: Susquehanna University Press, 1996), cover fly summary statement.

26. Paul R. Grim, " The Rev. John Rankin," 236.

27. Jonathan Earle: "Marcus Morton and The Dilemma of Jacksonian Anti-slavery in Massachusetts, 1817-1849," *Massachusetts Historical Review*, 4. N.A. (2002) 17-18. hhttp://www/historycooperative.org/journals/mhr/4/earle/html

28. *History of Tazewell County, Illinois* (Chicago: Charles C. Chapman and Company, 1879), 534.

29. Keith P. Griffler, *Frontline of Freedom*, (Lexington: University of Kentucky, 2004), xi.

30. Ibid., 93.

31. W.H. Siebert, quoting from correspondence from E.J. Holcomb and N.D. Ross in "Station Keepers and Their Methods," rough draft. Seibert Papers, Ohio Historical Society.

32. W.H. Siebert, interviews with Catherine Cummings, December 23, 1893 and Gabe Johnson of Ironton, Lawrence County, September 30, 1894.

33. W.H. Siebert, interview with Catherine Cummings, December 23, 1893.

34. *Ironton Register*, September 3, 1891, 1.

35. Keith P. Griffler, *Frontline of Freedom*, 93.

36. C. Robert Leith, *Follow the Furnaces*, (Funded by Lawrence County General Hospital Medical Staff, 2005.)

37. Virginia Bryant, Ironton historian, determined that John Rankin wrote his autobiography not at Ironton but at Vesuvius Furnace where the Gray Family, his granddaughter, was living at the time.

38. John Rankin, *Autobiography*, 40.

39. "Rankin Room" brochure, Lawrence County Historical Society. Ironton, Ohio. n.d.

40. *Ironton Register*, March 25, 1886.

41. *Ironton Register*, September 12, 1912.

42. *Cincinnati Times-Star*, June 13, 1931, 3.

43. *Journal of Social Hygiene*, vol. 28. (March, 1942), 151.

44. *Cincinnati Enquirer*, September 1, 1943, 7.

CHAPTER 11

1. *Tribute to the Life and Memory of the Reverend John Martin*, compiled by Jennie Martin Wilson, Hartington, Nebraska, February 3, 1905, 2.

2. Ibid., 13.

3. Ibid., 20.

4. *Ripley Bee*, May 16, 1906, 1.

CHAPTER 13

1. Carlton J. Corliss, *Trails to Rails, A Story of Transportation Progress in Illinois*, (Chicago:1934), 30-31.

2. Richard Cloyde sold 200 acres of Hensley Township to Washington Campbell on October 24, 1855, (Grantee Index, Champaign County, Illinois), 29.

3. Ralph D. Wilson, *An Engineer's History of the Boneyard Creek in Champaign-Urbana, Illinois(1830-1978)*, (Champaign: Ralph D. Wilson, 1978), section 2, 1.

4. U. S. Census, 1860, 6th Ward of Syracuse, NewYork, 85 Richard Cloyde.

5. DAR, Cemetery and tombstone records all show that Eleanor Jane Campbell died in 1856. The DAR records

show that daughter Eleanor W. Campbell also died in 1856. The cemetery records show that Eleanor W. Campbell died in 1858. Neither the cemetery records nor the DAR records have a listing for Elizabeth D. Campbell. Still, her name is on the tombstone and she is listed on the 1850 census as the oldest daughter and child. The cemetery records show that Eleanor W. Campbell was born in 1839. The tombstone and census show she was born in 1838. This research concludes that comparing the dates given in the various records against the latest census for the family, the tombstone is the most complete and accurate record of when and who were buried at Mt. Hope Cemetery.

6. *The Urbana Union*, Urbana, Illinois, March 20, 1856.

7. Henry Clement and John Clement of Warren County, Ohio, March 13, 1857, Deed Record Book L, Champaign County, Illinois, 762.

8. U. S. Census, 1860, Champaign City, Champaign County, Illinois, 634-635. Hired hands were Peter Kelly, John Black and John Ausinbaugh.

9. Washington Campbell held mortgage against Henry Fink, May 11, 1857, Scott County, Iowa, Grantor/Grantee Index, vol.7, Mortgage Book L, 1857, 131.

10. Supreme Court for the State of Iowa, Reports of Cases in Law and Equity, Edward H. Stiles, ix (Ottumwa:1872), 305-308.

11. James T. Lane, Attorney, correspondence to John M. Campbell, December 28, 1870.

12. The determination that a portion of the land of Washington Campbell became the Memorial Stadium of the University of Illinois was determined from close examination of the map of the city of Champaign in 1863. The map clearly shows the relationship of what once was to what not is. To verify this conclusion the map and the question was submitted (November 13, 2006) to the archives of the Urban Public Library. Carolyn Adams, archivist, did a close examination

of the property involved and concluded, "It does indeed appear that part of what had once been land belonging to W. Campbell is now underneath the Stadium."

13. *Union Gazette*, January 6, 1869.

14. Eliza Ralston (aunt) Probate Will, Brown County, Ohio, file #1462, December 19, 1891, lists Caroline Greenhagen of Hoquiam, Washington.

15. Eloise Campbell, interview by author, June, 1984.

16. Julia Johnson, interview by author, September 4, 1982.

17. Olive Harris, correspondence to author, 1992.

18. Eloise Campbell, correspondence to author, October 16, 1982.

19. Julia Johnson interview by author, September 4, 1982.

20. Tax Assessment, List of Taxable Personal Property, County of Champaign, 1872.

21. Celia Snyder, "History of Hensley Township," Champaign County, Illinois Genealogical Website. hhttp://wwwrootsweb. Com/~ilchampa/towns-townships/hensleytwnshp.html.

22. James Robert Crouch, interview by author, August 13, 1982.

23. Julia Johnson, interview by author, September 4, 1982.

24. Leota Campbell Knowlton, interview, recorded in *The Last Pioneers*, by James A. Campbell, (Dunlap, Iowa: 1984), 14-15.

25.   James A. Campbell, *The Last Pioneers*, 15.

26. Eloise Campbell, interview by author, 1998.

27. U.S. Census, 1900, Champaign County Illinois, John M. Campbell, Hensley Township, James M. Campbell, Champaign City.

28. Eloise Campbell, interview by author, 1982.

29. Arlo J. Campbell, *The Story of My Life*, (Pueblo,

Colorado: 1990), 14-15.

30. James A. Campbell, *The Last Pioneers*, 97-101.

31. Eloise Campbell, interview by author, 1999.

32. Dr. Allan Campbell, "Life's Reflections," August, 2006.

33. Dr. Allan Campbell, quoted in *Spurlock Museum Newsletter*, Spurlock Museum, University of Illinois, (Summer, 2006), 6.

34. Grace Micetich and Robin Fossum, *Spurlock Museum Newsletter*, (Summer 2006), 6.

Printed in the United States
79260LV00006B/6